Return to a Certai

Return to a Certain Region of Consciousness spans a poet's life-long dedication to poetry. To read it is to see what luck a poet must have to stay the course of a precariously unguaranteed adventure. Hankla never shies away from poetry's ravishing challenges or excuses herself from looking truth in the eye.
—Dara Barrois/Dixon, author of *Tolstoy Killed Anna Karenina*

Imaginatively free and endlessly inventive, Cathryn Hankla's poems have had from the beginning a sensibility all their own. Descriptive fluency and intimacy with nature are part of their wonder—they actively engage with the truth that humans "are not the whole planet / but neither are we nothing"—while Hankla's inquisitive, thoughtful, entertaining voice is another. Exploring regions of consciousness that range from a Luna moth's to the galaxies', Hankla's body of work has deepened and become more refined as it has grown.
—Carol Moldaw, author of *Go Figure*

To read Cathryn Hankla is to be reminded of what poetry is for. In her capable hands we are ushered into another's world to find ourselves more truly and more strange.
—Robert Schultz, author of *Into the New World*

At long last, readers can see the full scope of Cathryn Hankla's extraordinary poetry career in a single volume. *Return to a Certain Region of Consciousness* offers a thrilling portal into one of the most distinctive bodies of work in contemporary Southern and Appalachian poetry. This book brings Hankla's evolving vision into clear focus. She writes beautifully about people in near and far places, landscapes, animals, memories, and colors: "Forget me not: blue water, / blue breath, bluebells along roadsides, / dogs rolling in blue mysteries. So, no, /this is not Xanadu, but here there is the blue." Her poems move deftly through formal experimentations with prose poetry, double columned lyric meditations, and even very short poems with long lines, one of which reads in its entirety: "This is a heart trip not a head trip." Hankla has created unforgettable poems for more than forty years and *Return to a Certain Region of Consciousness* brings together the tightly woven strands of eleven poetry volumes into a single luminous tapestry.
—Jesse Graves, author of *Merciful Days* and
Tennessee Landscape with Blighted Pine

BOOKS BY CATHRYN HANKLA

POETRY

Phenomena
Afterimages
Negative History
Texas School Book Depository
Poems for the Pardoned
Emerald City Blues
Last Exposures
Great Bear
Galaxies
Not Xanadu
Immortal Stuff
Return to a Certain Region of Consciousness

FICTION

Learning the Mother Tongue
A Blue Moon in Poorwater
The Land Between
Fortune Teller Miracle Fish

NONFICTION

Lost Places: On Losing and Finding Home

Return to a Certain Region of Consciousness

New & Selected Poems

Cathryn Hankla

MERCER UNIVERSITY PRESS
Macon, Georgia

MERCER
UNIVERSITY PRESS

Endowed by
TOM WATSON BROWN
and
THE WATSON-BROWN FOUNDATION, INC.

MUP/ P710

29 28 27 26 25   5 4 3 2 1

Books published by Mercer University Press are printed on acid-free paper that meets the requirements of the American National Standard for Information Sciences—Permanence of Paper for Printed Library Materials.

Printed and bound in the United States.

This book is set in Adobe Caslon.

Cover/jacket design by Burt&Burt.
Cover art: Photographic Drawing 80, by Robert Sulkin, used with permission.
Library of Congress Cataloging-in-Publication Data

Names: Hankla, Cathryn, 1958- author.
Title: Return to a certain region of consciousness : new & selected poems / Cathryn Hankla.
Description: Macon, Georgia : Mercer University Press, 2025. |
Identifiers: LCCN 2024045659 | ISBN 9780881460414 (paperback ; acid-free paper) Subjects: LCGFT: Poetry. Classification: LCC PS3558.A4689 R48 2025 | DDC 811/.54--dc23/eng/20241001
LC record available at https://lccn.loc.gov/2024045659

CONTENTS

NEW POEMS:

Skydiving with Aunt Margaret   3
Shedding Antlers   5
Roll Back   6
Acorns   7
Before and After   8
Beggars   9
Lucky   10
A Willing Assistant   11
Bee Longing   12
The Livers   13
Full Moon   14
History of Splinters   15
Boomerang   16
Boom-harangue   18
Clues   20
Instructions   21
A Certain Stillness   22
Appalachian Sacrarium   23
Blue Dawn   24
Life List   25
Summer of Chiggers   26
The Donkeys   27

SELECTED POEMS (2023-1983):

From *Immortal Stuff* (2023)
All This Going On   31
Black Pepper   32
Divine Mushroom   33
Encores   34
Frogs & Toads of Virginia   35
Gettysburg   36
Giant Black Bear   37
Head Trip   38

HeLa   39
How to Tread Water   40
Immortal Stuff   41
Lesson #3   42
Marsupial   43
My Beggar   44
New Testament   44
Odder   46
Paper Sack   47
Puma   48
Recipes, Logistics   49
Saving Lives   50
With Sticks   51

From *Not Xanadu* (2022)
Autoethnography: Roses   52
Cinquain Sonnets   53
The Ravishing   55
Roanoke Logperch   56
Four-Chambered Heart   57
My Treasure   59
In the Garden   60
Washing Mother's Clothes for the Last Time   61
Can You Draw out a Leviathan with a Fishhook?   62
Not Xanadu   63
10% Ghazal   64
Runner, Reversed   65
Where Waters Meet   66
Tree Frogs   67
River School   68

From *Galaxies* (2017)   69
The Labyrinth Galaxy   70
Some Assembly Required Galaxy   72
Eclipsed   73
Goodbye   74
Lonely Horse Galaxy   75
Cedar   76

Galaxy of Virginia History   77
Conquistadors in the Colonies   78
Bee Tree   79
Galaxy of the Fathers   81
90-day Wonder   84
Galaxy of Waiting   85

From *Great Bear* **(2016)**
Another Nest   87
Brush Fires   88
Yellow Kayak   89
Root Vegetable   90
The Histories   91
Blessings of the Black Madonna   92
Bus to Mnajdra Temple   93
Babies in the Ruins   95
The Sleeping Lady   96
Caravaggio's *Baptist*   98
Autoethnography: Weeping Cherry   99
Great Bear   100

From *Last Exposures: a sequence* **(2004)**
Abstraction from a Life in the Body   106
Not Having Read *The Poetics of Space*   107
Life on the Rocks   108
Laramie, or Our Town   110
Immanent Creation   111
When Leaving, No Reentry Permitted   112
Last Exposures   113
Home Movies   114
A Fragment of the Author's Manuscript in Her Own Hand, II   115
Five Minute Exposure, Large Format   116
Twenty Minute Exposure   118
Only Thyme   119
Kennewick Man   120
Ghost Family   121
Pepper, 1930   123

From *Poems for the Pardoned* (2002)
On Athena's Shoulder   124
Dancers at the Edge   125
Indian Pipe   126
Resemblances   127
Luna   128
A Variation on "The Roses of Saadi"   129
In the Belly   130
Sandstorm   132
Poem for the Pardoned   134
Buddha Going out of Business   135

From *Emerald City Blues* (2002)
Natural Wonder   136
The Just Normal   137
American Beauty   138
Apparent Miracle   139
Magdalen Deer Park, Oxford 1979   140
Snow Rose   141
Vanishing Lady   142
Fantasmagorie   144

From *Texas School Book Depository* (2000)
Did the Souls Go   145
Great Blue   146
Irrelevant Violet   147
Self-Reflection   148
Texas School Book Depository   149
Baby   151
Thinking to Scale   152
Civil Rights   153
Red Beets, Steaming   154
God Attack   155
Reading Simone Weil at a Tender Age   156
Baby, it's Cold Outside   157
Renovation   158
Mont Sainte-Victoire of the Local   159
Jackie is Dead   160

From *Negative History* (1997)
The Editing Room   161
Swimming Naked   163
The Visible Woman   164
Burned-Out House   166
Conversation, Mostly Blue   168
Long Roots   169
Hindquarters, Under Moon   170
Wounded   172
Broken Bucket   173
Underwater Photograph   174
Double Karma   176
Autopsy After Death of "Lightning Conductor"   177

From *Afterimages* (1991)
Double Drowning   179
Dear Friends   182
The Angel on the Ceiling   184
Woman Once Thought Dead Recovering   186
A Lady Writing a Letter by Vermeer   187
Lady Reading a Letter at the Open Window by Vermeer   188
In Focus   190
Flight Luck   192
Lighting the Dark Side of the Moon   194

From *Phenomena* (1983)
White Summer, Museum Street, Montgue Street in Winter   195
Earth & Apples   196
Mockingbird   198
Mothlight (1963)   199
Water Burning Wills Away   200
Volume 13: Jirasek to Lighthouses   202
A Wilderness of Light   204
Firefly   205

Acknowledgments   207

Gloria in Excelsis Deo

NEW POEMS

SKYDIVING WITH AUNT MARGARET

We were related again,
the dead and the mostly
living,

sliding layers of cakey
atmosphere, parachutes
blooming side

by side, our conversation
as improbable
as saying

to a mountain, *move*,
and its moving.
At a certain point,

with ground swelling
beneath us,
we had to separate

and sail free. Our riggings
might entangle us.
You cascaded fast—

I saw you touch and roll,
black and white
dress a tablecloth

whipping down
the green hillside. Your
alligator pumps

did not fly off. I knew
you were a goner,
but you died

years ago.
From this perspective,
as I fall, too,

the ground will be hard,
of course, but sky
is what covers us.

SHEDDING ANTLERS

It takes a lot of energy to grow antlers,
she says, having taught a group of kids
to discover nature. Did you know
that, Cuz? Not the part about creatures
gnawing the shed for essential nutrients,
I say. Does nothing exist without
purpose in the forest, superfluous,
maybe just for aesthetic bliss? The silence

between us suggests we are both thinking
of the waste of her son to a gun while he slept.
Meaning makers, yet nothing with us humans
is so easy to find logic in or collective benefit:
Something falls off the crown of the head
to keep another animal breathing.

ROLL BACK

Let's go ahead and roll it back to see you climbing out of the womb face up. Let's review the record to check if you cried over spilt milk or manipulated, playing one who raised you off the other. Lucky you, you got two. I understand you'd rather just go forward, but I'm afraid you must occasionally offer reflection, because *we*—I can't reveal exactly *who*—have to review your personal file. All the tapes. It's our job to do so. Your rights have not been violated, so forget about taking action against us. Okay, now that we understand that this must happen, and probably will happen again, what can you tell us about what we are seeing on the see-saw? How would you describe your reaction to your first seven years of formal schooling? Your speech is sort of highfalutin. What happened in high school with the biology teacher? Have you individuated from your family of origin? Quick, justifications carry more weight if cogent and unrehearsed: First marriage? Job performance? Wanderlust? In your own words, of course. Caring for others? That's big with us, even a metaphysical marker. Can you make a case that you've sufficiently supported others without abandoning yourself? Next, have you strictly followed whatever plan was communicated to your personal internal monitoring system and not deviated despite your designated path being laden with difficulties and others questioning your actions or motives? You are not speaking fast enough, so I want you to know that I've had to leave some blanks. I can't tell you the consequences of my leaving blanks, but there will be consequences.

ACORNS

With no particular rhythm, acorns pelt the apex of the roof, roll, and rattle the gutters. In the middle of the night, I want you to see it my way, not as a promise but as all possibility. Perhaps at dawn when the random punch of acorns slows like popcorn in its popping, or when you too abandon sleep and go rambling through the house.... You'll say it's for a glass of filtered water or a bathroom break. Perhaps, there is a place where your bare feet meet my brokenness. Ready for an Australian shepherd to work fur-lined slippers like sheep, line them up, repeat? Here we are in the morning, combing through options with more fervent delight.

BEFORE AND AFTER

The middle of the bed is where I sleep. Sometimes I throw my arms around a pillow.

BEGGARS

Muzzle gripped by a twitch
                    as a garden hose

irrigates the open
                    wound, the quarter horse

stands and takes it, restrained
                    by another pain.

It makes sense this season
                    to turn toward the breath,

not sling yourself forward
                    out of old habits.

If wishes were horses—
                    we know the riders.

But we are all beggars
                    with no wish to choose.

Stalwart, my coat ashine,
                    standing staunch and still,

I hole up in my mind
                    flinching no muscle.

LUCKY

American crushed-breast
              robin, turned up rust

to sky. Unnatural
              exposure of heart,

wings to asphalt, darkened
              by contrast. White wisps

of feather—Red gash marks
              the absolute worst

our world can do. Windows
              above this felled one

tell the story: Flyer
              unable to see

a difference between
              sky and glass, mate

and threat. This downed robin,
              such small transcendence.

Where a sign for luck once
              shone, a grief all mine.

A WILLING ASSISTANT

The woman's cut in half
                    in the magic act.

Locked in boxes, she lies:
                    "It's not you, it's me."

The magician adjusts
                    his tailcoat before

donning white gloves to saw.
                    It depends on him

to find the slit and miss
                    the compartment where

she twists torso and bends,
                    flipping her limber

legs out of reach. Buzzing
                    deafens them both. Hush

now, hush, crying baby
                    in the audience.

Her body won't be harmed:
                    Hearts will split in two.

BEE LONGING

Crawling the battlefield,
                    trapped borer bee grips

brothers, sisters, implores
                    eyes to eyes, shining

dark bent fractals. I can't
                    pretend to love much

about these plump slow
                    bees trailing sawdust

to mark fraught tunneling.
                    This carpenter bee,

entranced and entrapped, crawled
                    in eco-seeking

to lay its eggs, instead
                    it will join these dead.

But this is my home—This
                    boundary means we

live here now, yet brother
                    buzz must be with us.

THE LIVERS

Prometheus, you knew
               what would come for you.

Maybe not at the start,
               Olympic fire

blazing your heart, arm held
               high with the torch, bold

benevolence bursting.
               But soon the eagle

would make its cruel brunch.
               Part of you, of me

filters what's given us,
               reclaiming some sense,

recycling toxins,
               spinning gold from grief,

order from confusion.
               Our daily quests:

I recount syllables.
               The raptor rends flesh.

FULL MOON

for Richard

When they carried you out
                      under a full moon

the black bag did not glow.
                      They said they might stop

halfway down the concrete
                      steps to rest, but they

didn't. Dave said, "He's not
                      heavy." Asked, "Is he

a veteran?" Turned the
                      satin cover to

the side without the flag.
                      If there were an Art

flag, petals the blanket,
                      blowing down signals

of new shoots and shining
                      in glory, in moon-

light—This is how we move
                      our bodies at last.

HISTORY OF SPLINTERS

There were more splinters than they had imagined, but not as many as they had feared. He had a splinter and then she had several. They both had them embedded in their right hands. They were both right-handed. They would have to dig them out with their non-dominant hands if they didn't seek help. This seems to be something special, the non-dominant hand thing. There's a book about drawing that touts drawing with your non-dominate hand. Maybe if they had done more of that sort of drawing, they'd be ready for this moment. And drawing things upside down is also a big thing. I'm looking at my splinter upside down and it still looks like a damn splinter, but if I have to dig this thing out upside down with my left hand, it's not going to be pretty. The thing about splinters is that you try to minimize the damage as you pick along with your needle. If a lot of blood oozes out, you can't grab the exposed end with your tweezers. It's about timing as much as slippage. When I was a kid, I scooted bare feet across an oak floor and came up with a giant splinter. I learned how much courage I had, and how much trust, letting my aunt dig into the meat of my sole.

BOOMERANG

Magic rocks off   and miserable
ways to make yourself inviolable.

Step backward   try to launch
into cerulean as a bunch

of green walnuts pelts your lunch.
But really that's enough

smoking chimps in the trees
of this mind freeze.

Turning leaves are inflected
with orange no more than expected

in this outback year   which is
bushwhacked and blessed.

No longer marking the calendar
day by day on my star chart.

Cartwheeled and descended.
Can we just say *ascended*?

Let's watch from the roof
as some whirling Sufi

moon waning   meteors over
between bouts of thunder.

I monkey groom your coat
which is to say I've got

eyes to see and they ache.
All that I notice won't slake

my thirst for beauty   weary
with shit I wish not to see.

I'm like those three   See Nope
Hear Nope   and yet I speak. Oops.

BOOM-HARANGUE

In the old days with the dial phone
five numbers for everyone.

When school was over
Barnabas Collins was my savior

Dark Shadows forbidden elsewhere
but not at my house with the were-

wolves ordinary and the war angst.
I could sit pillowed amongst

vampires' generational curses
decoding parental distances.

Such desolation   I grokked.
Some issues would always lack

resolution   staples of my vital ground
my Transylvania. I promised to sound

a gong   make like a puny paragon
didn't I? Did I? That song   that son-

ogram. Back then we didn't have them so
they never knew I was another girl until too

late. I lay wrapped   cheerful creature
without proper noun or nomenclature

in a world where *to hack* took a cleaver.
Beaver had an older not as dorky brother

post A-bomb and napalm   that portmanteau
of the real-life horror show

but who can remember his name?
It's beside the point   Wally   that I can.

CLUES

I've shed DNA everywhere from the coffee bar to the compost bin.
The guest bathroom teams with it. A researcher could get the wrong
idea, but I didn't sleep in your house much less your bed and am just,
sort of, at best, a housesitter. Books cover your bed, upon which you
remarked, and afterwards stacked them neatly before leaving, but I'm
not an inquisitive person—I don't know their titles. However, there's
an embroidered pillow in the living room, "I cannot live without
books," so books must furnish us a theme. Your black dogs are also
away, that's how unofficial I am, so strike that about a theme, please.
I don't even know enough to say definitively that the decorative urn
in your bedroom beneath the window contains your wife's ashes. The
drama of light was not where you'd expect last night. Cloudy and
drab the sky overhead, but the fields down toward the creek were set
aglow, all singularity, with firefly clues flinging this way and that,
stuttering up and jotting down, or spun sideways like crab-nebula.
Sometimes the spectacle of the heavens isn't what it's cracked up to
be, and you have to look for compensatory lights in the trees.

INSTRUCTIONS

These boots are for hiking.
>Hike only in these boots.

This is a water bottle.
>Fill this bottle with water only.

If you encounter a bear, do not run.
>Back away, singing a national anthem.

These are sunglasses.
>Wear dark glasses only in the sun.

Do not touch any leaves of three.
>Don't argue with me.

This is a cell phone.
>Use it only in emergencies.

This is a butane camping stove.
>Do not improvise with other fuels.

Look for evidence of frogs leaping off logs.
>Don't look for actual frogs.

This is a dammed, manmade lake.
>If you want to swim, dive in.

This is a book of poems.
>To read poems, open this book.

Listen for birdsong.
>Don't ask what kind of birds keep singing.

A CERTAIN STILLNESS

Ring finger empty for years.

Blue chicory sprigs on the grassy path.

Between Paris Mountain and Gallion Ridge, this valley.

Grasshoppers stagger in the wake of a hiker.

In the distance opposite the firepit, five houses bloom.

Occasional engines disturb the dark ribbon.

A lone deer munches not far from McDonald's Mill.

Helicopter buzzes over the high field.

Berry-speckled scat on the pier—Did a bear dive in the pond?

Grave of a friend, a friend to all.

Around my faded red chair, a tiny monarch circulates.

A bee lights on my ring finger.

APPALACHIAN SACRARIUM

Scarred blue walls adorned with figures of harvest and herding: 86 square feet unearthed, a sacred room. Oyster shells cast into a pile in the corner spell Roman virility and when ground to powder, plastering ingenuity. Civilizations can erupt between heartbeats. My folk wisdom radar is mired in poke ink, ink shed for thee. Mountains riddled with deep pits and a history of cave-ins rise above a table set with bagged salad. Kale, the king. No ramps or dandelion greens. What does it mean to be born in a place? A place extracted, vanished, and vanishing. Seriously, you can't choose your people. Everything named is ripe for stereotyping. Say your word for grandmother without revealing where you came from. Say Redbud and Mountain Laurel, say come to find out, say yesterday, say church or temple, cathedral or mosque; say pintos with chowchow. Say they fell away, say something real about how you were raised, say hello, cornbread; say pop, say fetch me the, say Cumberland Plateau, say box turtle, dulcimer, coal-dust-covered go-go boots, that's irony for ya. Say shale walls snaking death curves, say tipple; you can't say goodbye, so say fare thee well, until we meet again where the rose grows "'round the briar." Say fixin' to. Dreaming up ways to thrive from your front porch swing. Say, you've never been anywhere but in these here hills all along.

BLUE DAWN

It's true a tiny blob of Dawn detergent and a little scrubbing removed watermarks from one of my shoes, running shoes I wore to walk through dewy grass among headstones in the cemetery where my paternal ancestors and my father are buried. Today, I'm wearing the same gray shoes to walk through another cemetery, the final resting place of my maternal ancestors and my mother's cremains. I bought a niche for myself near my mom's. The cost of engraving was included, they said. Another member of my family was buried here this year. A few months ago, a scar of red clay marked his grave and a yellow plastic flag flew: "NEW GRAVE SPECIAL CARE." His name was handwritten on the flag in fading ink. This morning grass weaves over the broken flagstick and shines in the sun, still wet. I look down at my running shoes and see watermarks returning, this time to both shoes.

LIFE LIST

Before the piping plovers came to nest—
returned mid-May to roost in wrack—you left.
These shorebirds winter southward, where've you flown?
Beachcombing, your long legs shone like seafoam,
your face delighting in ruddy turnstones.
I've loved the mystical ibises best—
In trees like paper lanterns, brilliant moons,
they hover marshlands, lift away as one.

While sanderlings race to keep tridactyl
feet dry, I'm shaking sand from sandal straps,
remembering your endangered life list.
A mourning dove flushed up from the inlet,
out of synch for a moment, perches close
to me, cooing, a breath from leaving us.

SUMMER OF CHIGGERS

I first heard of the chiggers from my cousin. She said she had them or had had them. Then a friend might have mentioned them, but I hadn't heard of chiggers since I was ten, so I paid no heed or attention. Other people had chiggers or had had chiggers over the intervening years, not I. Out in my backyard, the walnuts were piling up. I tried raking the green lumps with the falling leaves and dumping them into the city's Big Blue with my bare hands or scooping them with a spare dust pan. I hurled green meanies into the bin one by one. This method produced the most conclusive sound. When Dave said he had chiggers and couldn't get rid of them, I was skeptical. A red bumpy patch had erupted on my side that I'd attributed to poison ivy. It itched like hell and hadn't responded well to various expired medicines. "What could this be?" I asked him. When I asked Rachel how her summer went, she told me she'd contracted ringworm from her visiting granddaughter. I hadn't known what to say to Rachel, but now I said to Dave that I might have ringworm. I knew enough to know that ringworm wasn't really a worm. "Looks just like my chiggers," he said. He'd had ringworm in college and blamed it on a one-night stand. He explained the unseemly nature of the invisible beast we were dealing with, "They are mites. They poop in your skin." Then he added, "I have the prescribed ointment right here."

THE DONKEYS

Donkeys follow me with their eyes. I knew it would be like this. They think they might like what I'm eating, but I know they wouldn't. Three not so wise little donkeys, non-ruminants like us but herbivores, they would be ecstatic chewing grass if I were not scarfing smoked salmon. Donkeys are the flesh and Jesus the riding master of the spirit. These donkeys witness my supper. I've had my personal crucifixion, my phoenix rise and fall again. The last sip of bourbon mingles with a chunk of ice that melts slowly on my tongue. Dying this way, donkeys and all, wouldn't be a bad way to go.

SELECTED POEMS

(2023-1983)

ALL THIS GOING ON

Some people clenched their jaws at night, while others kept on bruxing. They indicated winds were coming from the west, cold chills and then hot dry breath. A mixture of aggravation led to increased feelings of buoyancy. But it was more like buoys bobbing than a helium ascent, together with feelings of inferiority and a sandstorm of curiosity. We couldn't see much that wasn't distorted by high or low angles. Even a fisheye ceased to yield perspective. Individuals took walks now and then or volunteered for the army. Crowds seemed inevitable. Feelings of anxiety elicited a prescription for outdoor unity, marches, protests, and a change of the national colors from beige to hot pink, black, and gold. Me, I just wanted a dog like the old one, certain of himself and containing multitudes, everything from spot-skinned spaniel to wiry schnauzer—and, as I've said before, a perfect gentleman.

BLACK PEPPER

My cat, Tiger, standing tall on hind legs, toppled me when I was two.
One of my high-tops got stuck in a cinderblock. At four, I glued a
cotton bunny tail on construction paper and called it a placemat.
What Mother kept I can't throw away. Back then, I was fascinated by
adults who kissed. Black pepper looked like dirt flecks and stung my
tongue. I dodged red ash my dad flicked from his Kents. I've already
decided to give up *writing* so I can write. To give up protestation, so
the giant cat can tip me over. I'm no smarter than I used to be. When
I crack my head on the sidewalk, I cry. An honest reaction, but hardly
wisdom.

DIVINE MUSHROOM

I'm not sure about the dark orangey shells growing from the maple roots. They could be toxic or immortal (*Ganoderma lucidum*). Like sunshine or joy, reishi cannot exist without its shadow. Like the fungi, I think I might be here to imagine what it must be like to be here forever. My roots are shallow or deep, I'm not sure which, but I am immortal, too. My uses are few and unmeasured by scientific means. My mind wanders more and more and lands on growing things that are true in their own rights, springing up after rains, and have no need of my understanding to complete them, nor have they any use for appraisals of their worth. This is hard on some but becoming less of a burden, just as a shot of cold truth goes down easier on the gullet than the bitter green worm medicine my father used to spoon out to us at the end of every barefoot summer.

ENCORES

After "Rhapsody in Blue," there's little more to prove. The pianist rises from her bench to fetch some honest thunder, slips briefly into the wings and floats out again, Mozart awaiting. A large projection of her chubby, nimble hands looms over us as she doubles down in ivory. We applaud her again with every sincerity while inching toward the parking lot. But no, how could she cling like a wasp to its sting? We dive to reclaim our musical chairs as she attacks Ravel's "Concerto for the Left Hand," punctuating it with foot pedals, enlarging and enriching the sound. Oh, how her passion rips the air as we fidget! Paul Wittgenstein, elder brother to Ludwig, lost his right arm in World War I and commissioned Ravel (among others) to compose for him, so I know there are other such scores. After her third ending flourish, we rise and pound battle-weary hands, feet all but stomping. What? She doesn't even leave center stage this time but slyly squats again. *Whereof one cannot speak, thereof one must be silent.* "I'm done," mouths my companion, breaking the spell. I quickly trot after him. "They should have warned us," he says, pointing to the program. "She should have stopped while the left hand was ahead."

FROGS & TOADS OF VIRGNIA

Little green clinging outside the studio door, wedged in a shallow corner, nearly eye level. Someone called you a toad, but I know better. Your sleepy eyes could have winked at me but didn't. Little green, chubby, stubby, you remind me of the Luna moth I saw out on a limb here a few years ago. Same intensity of singularity, but you are dressed in a lime wetsuit, and the moth, upon closer inspection, was furry, wings so dusted that my touching them meant injury. Little green harbinger, you are not the only crawling or leaping thing I see today, but you are the boldest and the highest. You're probably a treefrog with your own distinct family, because no other frog can be this shade of green in our state unless you hopped a freight from New Mexico, and of that I am dubious. I have the chart before me, and you are nearly indescribable, off the map. Squirrel treefrog (*Hyla squirella*)? I love the name, but it's not yours. You're too large a climber. Green tree-something, my uncertainty of froggy, never toady, it's so natural to talk to you. Pinewoods treefrog *(Hyla femoralis)*? No chance of a color match. Barking Treefrog (*Hyla gratiosa*)? Possibly. I get out my dinosaur ruler but you wriggle higher, not making it beyond Plesiosaurus. Green treefrog (*Hyla cinerea*)? There is a river below us, but you would be even smaller and closer to the splash. Could you just be a common true frog of family *ranidae*? How disappointed by life would I need to be before saying YES? My choices are limited, and here you still cling, little green, sloe-eyed and determined.

GETTYSBURG

Lights dimmed on the diorama in the center of the room as a reenactment movie played. At strategic moments, spotlights illuminated the model battlefield. I didn't know exactly what I would find there, having traveled to Pennsylvania with my husband, whose penchant for violent history felt a little awkward. He had missed all the wars, but his father, like mine, had served in World War II. Between our fathers, we had both theatres of war covered. Side by side, we were startled by a resounding drumroll, a deep voice intoning, "And suddenly, *they* charged over the ridge!" And as completely errantly we found ourselves cast as Southerners; we played the others in this equation, rushing the hill on a fool's errand. The narrator was detailing the *high-water mark* of the Confederacy, Pickett's futile push over Cemetery Ridge. Until that instant, I had spent zero moments in contemplation of Southern heritage, and now I was drafted by a phrase into a romance with defeat. Other than having a taste for pimento cheese and iced tea, unsweet, I thought I had escaped indoctrination. Appalachians mainly went north in that war, with their sympathies if not their feet. But even *they* charged over that hill. Ambivalence stirred at the heart of my discomfort, along with a certain disgust at hailing from Virginia, my far southwestern corner conflated with the other end of the state by outsiders. Meaning, the capital of the Confederacy and defense of the indefensible belonged to me. Simultaneously, within the Old Dominion, my region had long been discounted, a target for the war against poverty and energy extraction. The lights came up around us. Blinking, we stepped onto the battlefield.

GIANT BLACK BEAR

You said the bear was of my making. Over me it loomed, or maybe it rose early in the evening as its own star deepening into its own sky. Stories above where I crouched, the giant bear occupied all of space, as I craned my neck to climb its height with my eyes then tucked my head to hide. I could hear it sniffing the air with a fee-fi-fo-fum. I pulled myself into myself to absorb my scent into my pores for fear the winds would betray me. I could smell my own fear, and I knew it would take only a few seconds more for it to waft. I couldn't hold my fear inside forever; soon enough it would attract the bear to me in a roar, each tooth larger than one of my feet, a mouthful of them shining in planet light. Toward me the bear turned, keeping its head high, and stepped over me, and went on stomping into the distance.

HEAD TRIP

This is a heart trip not a head trip.

HeLa

Henrietta Lacks was born Loretta Pleasant across the tracks in my
town in 1920. My mother was also born at home in the same town in
1918 and named Joyce. After being dropped in Clover when her
mother died, Henrietta had to plant and harvest tobacco until her
hands were sticky and stained. Growing up, my mother spent as
much time as possible in the public library, turning pages of books.
In college, she got a summer job there. Joyce and Henrietta both
married in 1941, one couple in April, the other in June. Henrietta
already had two children and would have three more. Ten years later,
Henrietta Lacks died from cervical cancer in Johns Hopkins hospital
the year my mother gave birth to her first child. Nothing touched the
pain Henrietta endured. Without her knowledge, her cells were
harvested and cultured for medical research. The HeLa immortal cell
line is still doubling and redoubling in test tubes around the world.
Both of the houses where Loretta/Henrietta lived in my town have
been torn down. The houses where my mother lived are still
standing. My mother died in 2016 of old age without any
grandchildren. I asked her to spit into a vial, so I could learn more
about my ancestry. She was skeptical but took the test for me. When
her results came back, they revealed mostly what she'd said, British
Isles. I have no idea where I'm going with this. There's really no
comparison to make between my mother and Henrietta Lacks.

HOW TO TREAD WATER

Jump in and walk from the shallow end until your toes can barely touch bottom. Bring your knees up and pedal a bike in the water while finning your arms back and forth. Come on, you can do it. If your head sinks under, stretch your toes toward the black stripe. Bounce up and try again. No, don't lean back floating, using that bubble in your swim cap, or you will be disqualified. The clock will start over. Ride the bike with your feet kicking in succession and let your arms smooth the water. After a while, you can do this and talk to your neighbor and forget about technique, but stay in one spot. Don't swim, or you will be disqualified. The clock will start over. Remember, the first rule is to save yourself. It's like running in place, someone said, standing over us, god of the pool deck.

IMMORTAL STUFF

The physicist tells his audience we are made of "immortal stuff." He's not brash enough to say we are immortal, but he does say that all our hearts are pumping around iron particles that came from the same dozen stars. Then he says that every day you slough enough of your stuff through respiration, eating, hydration, and losing solids and liquids out the other end that it's like an arm a day goes missing. Every day, you regenerate a new 7%. After a year of this, he says, even your calcium and all but 2% of your fluff exchanges, just as four or five days from now your exhalation in Ohio will be helping a flower bloom in Belgium, and four or five days ago the air you are breathing left Okinawa. In other words, I'm thinking boundaries are illusory and already collapsing as two galaxies draw closer and closer, even if it takes billions of years, finally colliding and enveloping each other. This is why mystics tell us that whatever we exclude in the other we condemn in ourselves. There's nothing better than breathing in, breathing out, knowing giving is receiving, and rediscovering the wisdom of Keats, *beauty is truth, truth beauty.*

LESSON #3

I don't understand this table. I don't understand this coffee cup. I don't understand coffee. I don't understand the refrigerator. I don't understand yogurt. I don't understand frozen blueberries. I don't understand phones. I don't understand comic books. I don't understand the Bible. I don't understand toasters. I don't understand stoves. I don't understand clothes. I don't understand running shoes. I don't understand water bottles. I don't understand sidewalks. I don't understand cars. I don't understand exhaust. I don't understand faded yellow houses. I don't understand bridges. I don't understand West Highland Terriers. I don't understand people in shorts. I don't understand road signs. I don't understand bicycles. I don't understand policemen on motorbikes. I don't understand sewer systems. I don't understand grass. I don't understand swing sets. I don't understand vagrants. I don't understand children. I don't understand white people. I don't understand Black people. I don't understand little free libraries. I don't understand benches dedicated to dead people. I don't understand trees. I don't understand the dead. I don't understand runners standing still. I don't understand old people walking with canes. I don't understand amputees riding adaptive bicycles. I don't understand humming. I don't understand sweating. I don't understand sunlight. I don't understand air. I don't understand my body as my body. I don't understand my heartbeat. I don't understand how much of me is water. I don't understand who you are. I don't understand who I am.

MARSUPIAL

Laying beets in boiling water by their ragged marsupial tails.
Watching kangaroos bound from conflagrations that conclude a way
of being. Bathing their feet in balm and bandages. Peeling gritty beets
and staining my hands. Finding macropod joeys curled in living
pouches. Bringing everything to light one thing at a time.

MY BEGGAR

I was unlocking the door to the shop as the woman approached. She asked for spare cash. My hands were full. I said no. She walked on, her face contorted, a line drawing to which more shading was needed to make her fully dimensional. After work, I rolled my grocery cart through aisles collecting cans of beans and diced tomatoes, packages of pasta and meat, fruits, vegetables, various cartons. I paid at the checkout with plastic. At home, I unloaded the groceries and separated dry goods into the pantry, cold items into the refrigerator's compartments. Some friends buzzed and asked to meet for dinner. I decided to order the ribs, curly fries, salad with blue cheese dressing, a glass of red wine. My dinner cost almost as much as the groceries, with the exception of six bottles of wine bought in bulk to earn a discount. Our waitress talked too loudly, but I enjoyed my meal. As we were signing our credit card slips, my beggar approached ignoring my friends. She stood at the end of the booth in a holey hat and coat and asked me for anything I had to spare. I opened my hands and said I had nothing but plastic. My friends also said no, although she wasn't focused on them. Why not, I wondered, for any of us could have helped her.

NEW TESTAMENT

I have tried alternative paperclips, but metal is best. When you shake it, the magnetic paperclip box rattles and nothing falls out. My students like pink paperclips. My mother left a paperclip on a certain page in her New Testament. If I gave you a research paper, it wouldn't be right without a paperclip.

ODDER

What's odder than a groundhog but natural to a river? A tail winks—cotton on, cotton off; does the rabbit even see it? My rubber shoes pressure caesuras in grasses that pass stomach to stomach to stomach to stomach to udder. A stag leaps ahead of its hoisted jib. From the holt, cubs can venture, mammals after meat. Their HAHS mean halt and don't make them shriek. *For the teraphim utter nonsense...and wander like sheep*. What's slicker than a flicker and fetcher to fishes? What has the muzzle of a hound and the tail of a mink?

PAPER SACK

I've got nothing but a live chicken in a paper sack, its head sticking out. I cinch the wrinkly poke around its scrawny neck and carry it like that. Gravel burns under my feet, stuck between my soles and flipflops. I walk past some folks who see me shining like a ghost. I feed the chicken a few droppers of water during the day. Everything has a right to live, even if its ways aren't ours and its days are numbered.

PUMA

At the family farm you heard it shriek in the night. Numinous by
definition, it slunk the underbrush of unscythed hay fields, the feral
perimeters of an unfenced boundary. Limestone caves cored the land
beneath our view, and occasionally you'd come upon some scat,
check your guidebook, given pause. Your mother sprang things on
you from the vault of inappropriate family history. Off-handedly, she
thrust upon you a vat of scalding water you had to balance just so.
Then there was that time some hunters claimed they laid sights on
the black velvet face of a creature (*Puma concolor couguar*) whose tail
unburdened them of doubt, yet their shots missed. For me, the high
rim of a ravine above a creek was where it stalked, above the road,
above my car as headlights illumined a darkness not of the tawny
lion, an absence pointing to the thing.

RECIPES, LOGISTICS

My grandmother's penmanship lives on in recipes. She measured flour in a chipped teacup and pinched salt. My mother's poignant scratches are preserved on cards or letters. She mainly wrote thank you notes or apologies. My father's florid hand breaks the margins of letters he wrote to my mother and then had to censor, blacking out locations and logistics, because he was the chief communications officer on an aircraft carrier in WWII. I have several 3x5 notecards on which my father typed recipes for chemical compounds. Every now and then a letter goes silent.

SAVING LIVES

I am the lifeguard smelling chlorine every day. I am sort of in love with the other lifeguard. The pool manager is sort of in love with me. The three of us are rarely all here together. I sit in the lifeguard chair wearing a whistle, sunglasses, and a teeny bikini. It's always blazing hot without shade and miserable. "Afternoon Delight" is our favorite song at the swim club. Some people think sex will save them. I am occasionally distracted when some kid or parent comes to the lifeguard stand looking up to talk to me. They know better. They aren't supposed to break my concentration. Someone could drown. I scan the pool for weak swimmers. The water glares back. "Marco— Polo," kids never do anything but scream. They all sound like they are dying, but really, they are fine. I clear the pool with a piercing blast from my whistle, "Everyone out!" It's my ten-minute break, so I dive into the water to cool off. After a few strategic strokes, I climb out and wrap my towel around me. I choose an ice cream from the case. Somedays it's nutty buddy and some days dreamsicle. Whatever I eat comes out of my salary. I am employed after passing lifeguarding and W.S.I. (water safety instructor). An ex-army guy tried to sink me during the final. I passed because I remembered the first rule of life saving: Don't go in the water. I open the pool with a ring of keys and close it responsibly. I hop on my ten-speed to ride home, thinking about the other lifeguard I hardly ever see. This is the most exercise I get, riding back and forth every day after baking in the sun.

WITH STICKS

Autumn's sticks and withered leaves placed into the cauldron with a thatch of bark strips and a bit of faded lichen stuffed around a pinecone. It's called making a fire. At the store, I bought a bundle of split logs, because while you own a chain saw, I don't wield a long-handled axe. I select several white logs from the plastic sack and cinch the strings of my hoody. You take my hand, pointing out the waning brilliance above us as the moon climbs up through the tall oaks. With enough friction or one long match this girl scout arrangement will sizzle, and you can hand me a reason to be.

AUTOETHNOGRAPHY: ROSES

1.
Please, please
be less pale, I plead
my case to myself—
the boy's vigil
on the stoop,
my father's furious
gurgling at the boy—then
a man's voice on the phone,

cords blistered
from a Brooklyn parsonage,
says he's finally gotten over me.
We're both past forty—
my father's stone dead,
buried with his old-school purities.

2.
You sound funny,
little Appalachian girl,
like you're not that bright
and prob-ly a hillbilly
from up a holler or stranger
than—You sound dumb,
bet you can't play chess,
looks like you're going

to be paid less for working harder,
70 cents on the dollar.
A Black teen who studied Greek
still waits on the doorstep,
a dozen roses and thorns
rustling waxed green paper.

CINQUAIN SONNETS

THOU SHALT NOT

Before the falling taut, the blast. And next
the fire with human hands collects a kill
and offers meat to test what strength I've saved—
pinned butterflies inside until the end—
I know the flesh unblessed. But reach to eat.

I CAN'T

Fingers gnawing toward a lie find brittle
stems still nimble. Layers of mountain green
my eye, blue on blue, flowering into
hills, a last canopy as cirrus trill,
erasing themselves. I can't be a cloud.

FIGHT/FLIGHT/FREEZE

I kept my fingers tight inside my ears
to keep their fight outside my head. Smoking,
drunken, they'd swear. Swaddled in ghostly light,
I'd sweat in blankets summer nights, seeking
my place, a quiet, dark circumference.

WHIRLIGIG

I watch a maple whirlybird twirl by
miracle and muscle. Five times I've brought
the future on too soon or held the past
too long. Samaras, tree helicopters,
pelt me. I hold my breath and tigers bloom.

PARADISE ISLAND

The sun returns unchanged. Coconuts drop
or circumvent, but you are different.
Tourists squawk, parrots talk, and my question
waits unattended. Straw, jitneys, and conch—
you decide to wander. I shop and shop.

HONEYMOON

Night reprieves the shore, and lovers struggle
to see stars through muggy air, Jupiter
bright, brighter than Betelgeuse ever was.
Afterward, the sky receded from us.
Once home again, we flattened specimens.

DIVINING

Wind twists old sweetgums, global ornate seed
pods, fierce symmetries with S's for stems.
What is it about regret's swift ambush?
A split of branches divines water's seam.
I walk behind the rod, remembering.

THE RAVISHING

Christian mystics wrote of this,
the seizure that pours
from an opening shining toward
Mystery, poised for the Holy wafer.

A darter can be a diving bird,
or it can swim freshwater as a fish:
The soul searches its moorings
in angels or heretics.

Wandering the grass barefoot,
I stumble on rock, brush earth
and wind-tossed leaves from a marker
for the nameless unremembered.

ROANOKE LOGPERCH

King of the darters, your small body spans no more than
the length of my hand. Dancing fins splay along your spine
fanning coyly. Fancy feathered head dresses undulate as you,
insectivorous, shift clear waters, nosing gravels.
Narrow body tinted green, rimmed red at times
and slashed with generous tiger darkness,
someone transposed you into a public tank
where you sloshed until perishing.
Painting your lightening belly, I reach for yellow to distinguish
you from splashes startling your habitat.

FOUR-CHAMBERED HEART

Ruffed grouse, the longing in our four-chambered hearts
was matched, when you fluttered toward me as I sat,

beer in hand, on my deck. At first, I didn't get it.
You rounded my chair, dark collar and mottled tail imploring,

flexing, a banty dancer in fringed leggings and mask.
Circumnavigating, fanned tail waving its coal band—

or butterflies or a waterfall—puffy neck a black planet,
you drew closer, for reasons I did not understand.

I thought my ribs quaked over nothing, but you thrummed
for me, secreted in brush, and came a-courting.

The second day, your wings pulsed from my porch railings,
rising in volume and complexity, finally blurring

into love's purring engine. Hopping down to circle
my chair with practiced artistry, you hoisted your tail full sail—

my astonishment almost complete. On the third day
of your strutting display, worry turned me sullen.

You obsessed, proud crest erect. I knew I had to go away,
leave you for weeks. I prayed you'd find, in my absence,

a perfect mate. You argued, a-flutter and dipping and awhirl.
I tried to work it through as you entreated and swayed

alone, almost flying at me, swerving out of tune
before crashing back into wobbly orbit. Was I not moved

by such ardor? I hope you found her, yet I wait for
your return. I'll never forget you, ruffed grouse, or

your persistent drumming after what's impossible
in this world, but maybe not, in the next.

MY TREASURE

My feet find uneven ground shaved to dust by the blade.
Complete and bearable, my ache,
heart balanced on the scale.
My life, the broken egg and the living bird:
a blue jay feather is my treasure.

IN THE GARDEN

Tomatoes cling to withering
vines, outpacing split skins and chill.

At the end of the Republic
some voices are heard and some not.

Hasn't it always been like this,
your body only a seed pod

for what lies ahead? As Jesus
said, I will, like Jonah, arise.

They came, weeping, to tend his crypt.
He visited two Marys first.

I go out into my garden,
what's left of it giving last shrugs,

seeking now just powdery leaves,
places the light might linger.

WASHING MOTHER'S CLOTHES
FOR THE LAST TIME

The rinse cycle spins tangled intimates
like straw that must be spun night after night
into gold: her silk pajamas, my whale
hump bras breaching with camisoles and socks,
yellowed slips, abandoned feminine props.
In her final years all the primping stopped.
I polish her glasses as if she needs
to see. I don't know if she sees me here,

still trying to do anything I can
to interrupt the natural cycle
with a wager of care. I was never
the perfect daughter she treated me as:
my charms, ring, and labor traded for days.
Mother's wet clothes and mine wring together.

CAN YOU DRAW OUT A LEVIATHAN WITH A FISHHOOK?

My mother left her blood
in her Bible,
spilled from agèd hands
like wine from old vines.

It stained the Book of Job
when God's talking.
Most of the blood smear
covers *for ever*.

Dab a drop of water,
and a sermon
washes over me—
how little I know.

NOT XANADU

Tulip poplar turning leaves over in the breeze,
translucent mitts that know what it means to grow
when no one is looking. Ostensibly, every leaf
is a beginner, but that is enough to start

the bubbling that will blossom and surround
these leaves with color when the season breaks.
Azure means the blue of sky, an enormous idea

patched through. Forget me not: blue water,
blue breath, bluebells along roadsides,
dogs rolling in blue mysteries. So, no,
this is not Xanadu, but here there is the blue.

10% GHAZAL

Solar eclipse, August 21, 2017

What I could do with only 10% of the sun.
Write my first initial in the sky.

With 10% of you, I could work for ninety.
Write my initial backward in the sky.

Ten ants out of a hundred decided to march
up the back of my shirt.

10% of you might bring down an empire.
10% might change anything you want to change.

What I could do with only 10% of your attention.
Write my initial upside down in the sky.

Only one bee flew up my skirt
and left me professing its power.

10% of the light is more than I can see directly.
10% makes the day shine almost as bright.

RUNNER, REVERSED

Screeching rail cars, ties crossed and pounded,
moon halved and canted over the sign
of an electric company founded

in 1913. Where is the boy whose head
I cradled in my lap sometime in the 1970s—
a romantic gesture instead

of holding hands—whose dark curls smelled
of cigarettes toked by adults and faintly
of earwax, as he compelled

me to silence and recounted unbidden
that he had seen his mother shot dead
after she had been beaten

by his father, who then shot himself in the head?
Age two, waiting in the doorway, he
had no trouble, way past time for bed,

remembering every detail. I couldn't move
my legs beneath his mind that held
two violent deaths and proved

my experience limited to a ranting
self-dramatizing dad. Dark-haired boy
no longer cried about much of anything,

repeating his imprints in dull tones.
I pictured his house thicker than water
razed to rubble and stifled moans.

The coal cars searching for a place
pile up many engines, pulling together
toward a bend where all things trace

a path and pass on shining, multiple tracks.
Last of October's fireflies hover the grasses.
I wanted to run home afterward and act

as normal as possible at the table
of Mother's perfectly balanced meal:
one meat, a starch, and two vegetables.

WHERE WATERS MEET

Where South China Sea merges Pacific
we watch ridges of current rippling
nearly into flame as one pair of wings
entangles another, as one body
of water seizes its brother confined
in a sack of time. Grab my hand and gaze
over dangerous cliffs into whitecaps.
Earth is one organism, with humans

not the whole planet, but neither are we
nothing. I awaken each night hearing
or remembering metallic couplings,
coal cars and engines grasping hands of steel
far away from a meeting of oceans,
with you flung far from the music of trains.

TREE FROGS

Night-swimmers check pool
skimmers into which speckled
frogs have sucked, bunched up

green packages of
live matter without trumpets.
We stand by for jumps.

One ancient bullfrog,
front leg pinned by saltwater
and dissolving, waits

for rescue. We can't
save anything from ourselves,
not even barking

tree frogs. All our frogs
are barking frogs, our needs our
own. Don't make me leave

this one world, please don't.

RIVER SCHOOL

Admit me to the school of skittering
minnows and the raw skin of the sycamore

where silent, water-light movies play
beneath the leaves and limbs.

Admit me, legacy of the Alleghanian
orogeny with mountain origins,

to your twenty-four species of fishes,
especially the mottled sculpin,

fantail darter, wild rainbow and
brown. And in your highest tributaries,

above 1,000 feet, where temperatures
never reach seventy, the painterly

native brook trout, spotted spawning
mid-October, swifting deep karst pools

hemlock shadowed. Tiny shells
depositing oceanic spells bobble just

beyond my reach on the riffle bed
that reflects full branches in the heat.

Rowdy dragonflies raft an oak leaf;
their fraternity whirls past as I drift.

Admit me to the rites of the inner
tube and the privileges of being dunked

onto a ripple of rocks and hung up
in sunken trunks, ensnared by rooted fingers

of embankment. I float here knowing
that so much of this river's invisible,

as is love and all that means
anything to us, running underground

through limestone, coring caves,
firing synapses with a water mind

only to rise at Coursey Springs.
The green heron has been listening

from its high nest at the bend, as we
waddle like upside-down terrapins,

paddling finny hands and legs
in the currents of 300 million years.

THE LABYRINTH GALAXY

In the Labyrinth Galaxy one is always walking
in what passes for a line. One is possibly moving
along an impossible curve. It is standard
to trace circles and think you are not, as a rock sends water
in concentric waves when hurtled into a pond.
Don't let any of this distract you. The goal
is to be ever in motion toward your god. Keep going,
keep swimming and walking, whether you are to dance hot coals,
slog mud, or troll chest-high sludge. Don't look up unless you stop
altogether. Galay in your gaiters. Don't look down unless
you cough. The goal is to be ever in motion toward your god.
One jump will not do it. You must go around.
The spiral twists open while your eyes are glued shut.
You will meet your god in the present moment,
where the shape disappears, the journey collapses.
The goal is to be ever in motion toward your god.
You will meet your god near the sound of rushing water,
on a picnic bench surrounded by hedges,
as you sit with your legs comfortably crossed.

SOME ASSEMBLY REQUIRED GALAXY

It's not what you imagined, these
late nights of glue and limitation,

hands salt-sticky from snacks,
directions in three dead tongues.

You begin a Braille translation,
parts spread over the shred of rug

not puppy soiled. Setting aside
singular shapes, stacking baggies

of bolts, you time your breaks
to shaggy dog's piddles and poops,

convert to the church of the socket
wrench, metal screw, and wing nut.

Another month or year passes
while you buy the pictured tools,

matching a drill bit from aisle five,
bin three, to black lines sketched

in China. Now the old dog creaks.
You learn to navigate the alp

of stacked parts half awake.
And in the minutes between

dreaming and sleep, you work.
You work until you get it right.

ECLIPSED

Blinded by a chance at permanence,
via satellite I watch a sliver
of Alaskan sun,
wishing darkness could bloom.

To save your sight,
you follow the disarmed orb
focused through pinholes
or multiplied by leaves.

The lightshow dances
the grass, a primitive projection
so much like a marriage as it ends.
No one can gaze straight at the sun.

Cold echoes into spring
no matter where you are or who.
I drink from this glass, alone,
blotted again by the moon.

GOODBYE

The parrots say "goodbye."
Salamanders signal the health of a system.
Miners trust fierce
singing in the dark.
The parrot says "goodbye"
to the snow leopard,
spots vanishing into the scrub,
into the white dust
of our long winter night.
The salamander, shape-shifter,
signals the health of the system.
Let no one find you,
snowy owl.
Let no one track you,
mountain gorilla, sniff
your droppings, feed
on what you leave behind.
Parrots are costly
to capture and breed.
Salamander signals the health of the system.
So much depends
upon those changing colors.
The parrot says "goodbye"
in English, Spanish, and Chinese.
We've taught our parrot well.

LONELY HORSE GALAXY

"That horse is lonely," my father announced,
visiting the farm after my marriage collapsed.
Patriot kept chewing alfalfa.
I fed him cornhusks, apples from my palm,
petted him like the dog I'd given up.

"That horse is lonely," my father repeated,
leaning on the white fence, poking
his head into the field to focus
more poignantly on horse feelings.
Patriot trotted neither toward nor away.

"That horse is lonely." My father sighed
a big sigh. Am I going crazy, I wondered,
hasn't he said that before?
My father knew nothing about daughters,
a little about horses, cut off from the herd.

CEDAR

To hail from nowhere is a resonate gift.
It means you can be anywhere. It means I can be here.

Saw through the curved branch, fibrous
bark sinew-wrapped as wisteria vine,

and unseal the waft that will knock you down.
Its scent a bloodstain. Insect

proof. Divinely inspired.
To work with hands a length of life

into a shape of use is no small thing. My connections
fail.

The wood stuns me with power
even in dying.

GALAXY OF VIRGINIA HISTORY

"The worst insult in my thirty years,"
the teacher said. Arms flapping,
she turned from the board

to her brood.
Open on our desks, the Virginia History
fourth grade text.

Exhibit A: an ink drawing of a slave ship
approaching land,
brown arms and heads

poking from the hold toward air.
Exaggerations of smiling teeth
set for a birthday party.

The caption read:
arriving Africans "jumped for joy"
upon seeing

the Virginia shores…
In 1967, I raised my hand to ask
if those words were really fact.

CONQUISTADORS IN THE COLONIES

To be constantly reminded of who won the war.
To be constantly reminded that conquerors
are good, their intentions loving.

To walk outside and observe a couple of cardinals,
to listen to their song remembering
the appropriation of song, the suppression

of certain tongues, the oppressor's constant struggle
to overcome the cardinals, to locate their nest
before the eggs open. Or condition their children

to fly with their heads looking over their shoulders.
One flew backwards. One flew into a windowpane.
One could never learn. It was slow.

Someone said, "They're all like that."
Someone else nodded.

BEE TREE

A bee colony,
black hole
in a split juniper trunk.
Gnarled, rough mounds of bark
guard a slash of buzzing dark.

Wild bees delight,
work and hover—
dive into an artificial night.
They pass each other
to cover cones with stolen nectar.

This could be the last bee tree
in a food chain of cultivated
colonies. Bee homebodies
thrive—imports mingle
without improvement,

and migrants sicken, shipped
on flatbeds cross-country.
No swarm, only purposeful acts
in a daylong dance to and fro.
The gash of hive is low

on the trunk, the whole
secret two feet high.
This fir, bearing cones
like shrunken blueberries,
with bark striations of whitish grey,

resembles a faded fence post
more than a living tree.
Inside there is a kingdom
waiting to collapse
on a queen so plump with life

she cannot see the danger
of such sweetness. Expanding
honey cores the juniper,
as sinkholes honeycomb the comet's
nucleus until it cries out,

its coma burning bigger than Jupiter.
17P/Holmes explodes gas
and dust as sun strikes it.
To the eye, a fuzzy spot enlivens
Perseus. To the lazy

bees, tucked into a moon-lit tree
it is nothing. Soon, it is nothing.

GALAXY OF THE FATHERS

The fathers slog home from work tired,
ready for some chow.

The fathers are cheered in the uniform
of their country.

The fathers walk into a bar and order rotgut
shots in an Old West movie.

The fathers always earn their promotions.

The fathers return home injured, requiring
constant long-term care.

The proud fathers sport broad smiles.

The fathers take a day off and play golf,
bait a hook, shoot some hoops.

The brave fathers are decorated.

The fathers sacrifice their only sons.

The angry fathers decide to bail.

The fathers write a Declaration and sign it
with a flourish.

The fathers are afforded every opportunity.

The fathers take to the streets and grow
long hair.

The fathers are selfless.

The fathers are prayed to on a daily basis.

The fathers attempt some humor.

The fathers invade other fathers.

The fathers mutter about how everyone
is out to get them.

The fathers are anguished geniuses.

The fathers win large sums of money
for their *craft or sullen art*.

The fathers never have enough.

The fathers take medication prescribed
by other fathers.

The fathers say that standards are being eroded.

The fathers serve as final judges.

90-DAY WONDER

Something you had been meaning to say
a cause and a perfection
a reason for being
underwater
wearing a mask and snorkel
sailing by sextant
he almost failed navigation
in South Bend Indiana
two pilots downed in the waters
in front of the ship
it swerved to avoid them
but their charges
detonated upon hitting their depths
rocking the cradle
floating the dead
a cause célèbre
a plume of uncertain origin
on their shakedown cruise
just out of the harbor
they hit a whale
sixty feet in length
the bow sliced its spine twice
it came up in chunks
a bloody wake and some pieces of proof
they did not run aground
two pilots bounding across the deck
slo-mo bomb tilted from an enemy
wing
falling below the flight deck and into
unventilated quarters
of CVE-70
a little Kaiser's Coffin
well named at that moment

it takes five generations to produce
thunderous grease fires
blew unidentifiable bodies
in parts
sky high
one of the pilots kept running
without his head
the other one turned
and saw it
a war to end all wars
a shining example
that's what he was called
schizophrenic
of unseasonable warmth
the lake is usually cold this time of year
the ocean can change in a moment
wearing a belt and suspenders
I tried on his mid-shipman's
bell bottoms with button fronts
a shining example
of unwarranted affection
after twenty odd years
it strafes a village
it was nothing anyone wanted
the moths had left the wool alone
and nonetheless a suppression
above all else
Combustible Vulnerable Expendable
a 90-day Wonder
in a salty dog's war

GALAXY OF WAITING

Waiting at the firehouse doors,
enumerating hoof marks from a former age. Waiting
for steel wheels to flatten a coin on the rails,
so that it looks like a disk minted by eons of pressure. Waiting
for the Exodus and the Red Sea. Waiting for the reruns
of antiquity when returning gods favor the other side. Waiting
for laundry to wash then dry. Waiting for irony
to stop being so ironic, for cynics to rot.
Waiting for a taste of honey. Waiting for a taste
of the strong leaf tea of victory. Waiting for the lapse
of judgment concerning the past several centuries to abate.
Waiting for an end to sorrow. Waiting for inspiration.
Waiting for democracy to ring true,
pressed against the glass ceiling, under the harsh light
of yesterday, played again and again like there's no tomorrow.
Waiting at red for green promises. Waiting and waiting,
waiting for reason to prevail, waiting for planting season. Waiting
for the apocalypse and the white horses, and so forth.
Waiting for the cyst to shrink. Waiting for a phone
call, waiting for Christmas, the next stall, clerk, or straw.
Waiting for rebates, waiting for apologies. Waiting in pajamas.
Waiting in negligees. Waiting for the apiaries to buzz
again. Waiting for a stellar performance. Waiting
for a good series. Waiting for a drop in the bucket. Waiting
on rooftops for rescue. Waiting in 100-degree heat while the waters
rise around us. Waiting until some of us die and others
start wading through the muck. Waiting for the
alligators while we wrestle sharks. Waiting for plastic
to break down in the waters. Waiting for Exxon
to pony up for the spill. Waiting for reports
from the various branches which will confirm and support
what was previously suspected, accounted for,
and secretly installed as policy. Waiting for

an election. Waiting for lunch. Waiting for an oil change.
Waiting for some people to shut up and for others
to act up and speak up. Waiting for the kids at school,
parked on the circle with the other
mothers. Waiting for the bus after work with the folks
who take the bus. Waiting for that guy who always cracks
us up to do so again, while we're standing here, waiting.
Waiting for Walt Whitman to stop making so much sense.
Waiting for a raise. Waiting for a compliment. Waiting for an insider
stock tip. Waiting for others to stop whining. Waiting for
the rest of creation to see it our way. Waiting for the bootstrappers
to line up and just shoot the rest of us with
automatics, since we're so slow,
wasteful, and ignorant of the rules. Waiting for justice. Waiting
for just cause. Waiting for the Medal of Honor long after you're buried,
habeas corpus. Because you are an American Indian and all records
of your valor lost or incinerated, and the statute of limitations
has run out on your claim. Waiting for the horses to return,
and the firehouse doors to burst open
and a thunderous clattering ensue, pulling behind
it the answer to our many prayers, the water of conciliation,
the spiritual balm of healing, the baptism that feels like swimming,
the swimming that carries us all to the other shore.

ANOTHER NEST

I've pioneered the one person
conservancy, finding every gift that nature
never intended. Breath itself—no need
for music. Out in the sticks, I live silent
weeks with airplane's rip, creek's
slow revolution company enough.

No one else will see this perfection
in bark and plastic strips, molded
mud, spider webs, rag rug
strands wound into the globe
for a red-eyed vireo, a cup
in which to hide a tidy clutch of two.

Mid-winter the nest hangs bare, a shroud
of leaf twixt limbs not as thick
as my pinky. The missing vireo
cannot stand this weather. I check
the range map for a cold fact my mind
follows south to the Amazon basin.

BRUSH FIRES

I sit in trees, a place foresters call fuel.
The understory becomes me. Grouse and turkeys
know my sour moods, my sounds as I move
shuffling papers, searching pens.

A neighbor starts his clearing ritual, stippling
his arms with brambles. A thorn zippers
down his crown. His wife dabs
the seeping blood then offers a match.

The whole stack crackles at nightfall,
burns bright, rekindled. Anxious, I watch
the creek as it turns, the fire as it burns
on the other side, flame morphed to embers.

YELLOW KAYAK

A yellow kayak hovers on the grey drizzled river
beneath a swirling blizzard, flakes the size of swallows,
gliding slickly meeting elements.

Black paddles dip, balancing back, forth, east and west,
as a man in wetsuit traverses
long shelves of submerged geo-time paper-clipped with rocks.

A great blue heron opens one giant flap of wings
embracing low sky,
then dips toward shaggy edges where debris

hinges in every jag and scissor tooth of land,
blocking easy attempts at flow.
The white sheet edges higher on the body of the world

as I wait for Mother to stay or go
to surgery, and nurses, aids, and doctors cannot help
but search through windows checking dangerous roads home.

ROOT VEGETABLE

Another onion,
not a vine-ripened fruit,
neither plucked from a tree
but grown in the dark
like me, bound by clods.

THE HISTORIES

I lay my offerings before her:
silk musk of unveiled breast,
pots of fragrant ointments,
small color blazes,
a dipping spoon into sweet
or savory, salt and spice.

Hauled within the body
electric, shimmering
in an opalescent oyster shell,
we trace curry, coriander.
A ritualistic trek to the twin
orifices of desire.

The mouth of taking,
the mouth of giving.
Where we sink,
where we rise.
What has been said
or done we set afire.

BLESSINGS OF THE BLACK MADONNA

At Montserrat,
we climbed to a golden throne
that housed her, *la Moreneta*, earth goddess,
my way back.

What was sealed with her touch?
I asked for the standard healing.

Even the dead can be a consolation
after love. So, too, a wooden statue
lofting a ball. I
touched the sphere, her world

fell still. After love, the country
of origin surfaces
with everything once mocked,
its hollowness pocked with passion's failure.

What was sealed with her touch?
I asked for the standard healing.

On the way out I edged past
the many portals into people's pain,
replicas of legs, elbows, and breasts,
pictures of children, departed or living—

No one above blessing, no one below
saving. Irony is its own lone hell,
left behind for an hour, burned away
in the fires of seeking, the singe of feeling.

BUS TO MNAJDRA TEMPLE

Covering the blow hole
at his throat to speak,
the bus driver emitted

a mechanical syllable
to indicate the bus to Mnajdra.
I could see the fringes of flesh

quaver, and the snaking tube
that was his airway.
I could see the sea curling

blue along the shore
beyond the narrow cove
below the twisting road.

And when I got off the bus
I could see his scarred
hole, bare and rough

enough to incubate
the future, to serve as a nest
for incurable secrets.

I could see a hole carved
in coralline limestone
and the dark cubicle

where the oracle sat issuing
words to be unraveled,
words to be made flesh,

words that could traverse
these visible ruins,
the passage from the gut,

wind through the opening
to planet earth
and tell us our next stop.

BABIES IN THE RUINS

Among carved rock and mysteries
of scale, these mighty

ghost temples
fallen into disrepair—

built for a race of giants
who perished by 2500 BC,

built by farmers
with advanced sensitivity

to the afterlife and the fat goddess
of harvest, with no

metal tools, only stone axes
and imported obsidian blades—

come strollers, here and now,
pushed by parents from all nations

cooing and purring
into the cave of the pram

to their little gods
safe from the sun.

THE SLEEPING LADY

News from the Hypogeum: the lady
has been sleeping, who knows

how long. Longer than Dad
who began in 1999 and longer

than Grandmother who started in '83.
This sleep takes centuries

to conform to an hour. They say
she fell asleep in 3000 BC.

Layers of limestone sheltering
domestic animals, the calcareous

sheet, the deer, the pebbles
before the hippopotamus layer

and the bone-free clay beneath
have all been resting. Prying

up ciphers is a dangerous game, yet
here she keeps on her lighted throne

in the Archeology Museum, shrouded
by glass, protected by cameras,

unmindful, curvaceous, a small
clay figure more detailed than any

baby Jesus in the manger. This lady on
her clay bed has arranged her dress

for modesty as she takes the years
and winds them taut as drum skins,

spinning her story by night,
dreaming her world made flesh.

CARAVAGGIO'S *BAPTIST*

As the head awaits its final moment
of detachment, the saint's already fled alone,

no angel chorus background. Two prisoners
crane from their cell to gander the executioner,

whose muscles are meant for strength
not petty physique. Salome holds the silver platter;

the pretty courtier directs the henchman's last blow.
An old woman shields her face with clawed fingers

in this moment of shadow. The saint's eyes stare
open, and only his flesh is left to us

in this human picture, in this human place
of bones and limestone catacombs, clay shapes.

AUTOETHNOGRAPHY: WEEPING CHERRY

When I have drunk
too much wine and stumble
like any Chinese poet
to the base of a weeping cherry
in March, the damp ground
cold as a flat rock after dark,

a pudgy pilgrim in a shiny suit
wanders in from stage right
claiming some chicory from our yard.
His fist of blue weeds wilts,
torn half-hearted
from roots and spiny stems.

Blue bouquet collapsed before him,
he pounds our door, pushy
hummingbird slurping nectar
or fame's sticky elixir. Before
he wakes my napping new
husband, I confront this

trespasser, startling his reverie.
He is not looking for us.
There will ever be at least three
in this marriage plot. A stylized
water bug skitters a real creek
sucking life from the living.

GREAT BEAR

Bear burrows into my hand
as though I would let go—
I can't. In Ojibwa
Mukwa means Courage. Means
I'm left holding the bear. This replica,
copper-colored, humpbacked,
sprouts beady turquoise eyes.
I have seen black bears
shift country roads or juxtaposed
with suburban drives,
last gestures, untranslatable.

I need to bear up in the wake of loss.
Fine student, writer, friend, a year
beyond my age, now you lie beyond
this realm. Of the wool shawl
you gave me when my father
died, you said, *Wear the dull side.*
After a year, turn it bright,
go on with your life.
Fuchsia, turquoise,
yellow, blue, thin black
stripes—I take the mourning

blanket from cedar storage, drape
my shoulders as I cry. I slip
my feet into beaded deerskin
moccasins your aunt sewed,
a perfect fit. I sit for a while
at this desk and think. Arranged
in a slanted line, fetishes stroll on.
Wolf, because I was your teacher,
fertility frogs of all sorts,

and turtle, my consort.
So many gifts over seven years

of treatments, leaves of absence,
remissions. A leather medicine bag
of magic mojo accompanies
car trips. Safety and luck
for beginnings and journeys
appeared after I totaled the car
on a dusky road. My throat
almost closes when I conjure
your voice in my ear
calling, "Hey, Chief,"
calling me away from the living.

I cannot say how many days
your droll bit of reverence
kept me together body and soul,
head and heart attached.
I know what it is to be wracked
with diamond tears.
The sparkling Great Bear—
only the most prodigious
could flourish so far north—
stretches over my desk this night,
over my grief for you, Shelly, this life

of frail connection, little peace,
numbered days that test
most of us beyond our limits.
Small tokens of respect Shelly gave me,
one being to another, a proper
border crossing that clearly spoke,
I see you as more than

your function at work:
I see you, Chief. As her words
constellated pages, I tried
to help her generous gift speak.

I want to say, forgive me
for baring all. Artful evasion
would be best. I wonder
how such small glimpses
into lives outside classrooms
where we meet to study texts
can add up to so much.
I learned about Michigan, the res,
Uncle Toc, aunts,
father's alcohol, siblings' struggles,
from her stories. Her twin

sons share my birthday,
balanced on the vernal cusp.
I think of their losing her at sixteen,
just driving, just becoming men.
If not for her cancer diagnosis,
surgeries, chemo, recurrence,
given our combined reticence,
I would know even less.
In the Great Bear constellation,
eta Ursae Majoris—the last star,
blue-white, farther out

than 95 light years—is named
Benetnasch or Alkaid
and means "chief of the mourners."
Great Bear had the same name
in many tribes, Algonquin,

Iroquois, Illinois, Narragansett, Ojibwa,
and later, the Greeks. This sky
stretches over everyone
in patterns telling stories.
Astronomers say the dipper
shape will dissolve over time

into a plough. From water to earth,
we all make our journeys, breathing
between the planes. This passage
will take a minute or a century.
It's best not to think, to worry, to tilt
my head back too far angling
for transformation. To us the sky
looks stable, yet alive
with transits, orbits,
meteoric events. Each night
I take my chart in hand,

aiming to see more of what's real.
There's so much left, even as time
flits, tumbles, flips joy into
tumult. Artemis turned her acolyte,
Callisto, into a bear·to be hunted
after Zeus knocked her up.
Koans tell of killing teachers met
on the road, much more than
metaphor after Cho's gun.
These relations can be fraught.
As we stoke the mind's furnace,

emotions veer, troubled by
projections, by performance, by
in loco parentis, stirring ideas and lasting,

real affections. Bear with me.
In teaching, exchanges can
carry an alchemical charge.
Grandmother's brass bell sits
on my desk, relic from a one-room
school. Bound by titles
and protocols, we try hard
to make it all appear dutiful.

And when we read into another
through words on flat paper,
words half formed, barely conscious
of their power, we call
it responding, commenting,
or marking. We lower the stakes,
raise boundaries any way we can,
drawing sharp distinctions between our
mentoring and a shaman's work. Shelly
named me *Chief,* a humorous honorific.
Chief reader, critic. Now Chief

of the mourners. Students knock,
queue to show me proud scribbles.
Their lines, paragraphs, tracks
of symbols, scratches
in chiaroscuro sometimes
burn brilliant when clouds clear.
Will I be up to the task?
I fight down the urge
to make it more meaningful
than moments spent stoking a fire.
I get through the next session,

drop the humpbacked shape into my lap,
but it migrates back to one hand,
hibernates. I won't forget or let
this animal go. The next student asks
about the turquoise wolf. I won't
bear witness. Whose teacher now,
whose guide and trusted reader,
whose *Chief?*
One of the best is no longer
with us, all of her typing stopped.
Foolish, to think I could hold

them all like the carved bear, encircle
my clan with constant nurture.
I open Shelly's thesis
to read her story's end. A ghost
father appears in the apparition
of a deer from the mists
of Lake Michigan. Her struggle
took so much bearing down,
a push to the edge of ineffable
meaning that only rests in images,
which to explain is to destroy.

ABSTRACTION FROM A LIFE IN THE BODY

Any body can turn into a painted landscape
Or a page in a book. Flat planes are always
Ready to erase our dimensions,

As when we write half a truth and call it fiction.
The amount unknown, the vast interior,
Molten core and a million facts—

The man is lying on his back in a hospital bed.
Hourly, the x-ray machine hovers over his chest.
Soon the sheet will cover his head.

For now, he is breathing.
For now, I call him "Father."
In a few days his hand

Will draw away, his eyes will dull
On a point I cannot follow.

NOT HAVING READ *THE POETICS OF SPACE*

The pilfered nest rests easily on the palm,
Open to air, chicks departed.
Late summer, I remove it from the floodlight,

Arrange it on the ground
In an elbow of weathered wood.
I save the mud-crusted hollow, the divining

Twigs, stems, moss that was pressed to the breast
Curve of a Carolina wren. The bird's instinct
Will not return it to this twining—

Snow may fill this clever bowl—
Yet I have an instinct to preserve its story,
Written wisps of down, written sticks,

Bit of ribbon where hatchlings pecked through
Rough shell, and somehow flew.

LIFE ON THE ROCKS

The mineral green of desiccated seas
Spills down low hills, a mirage of grass
In an ocher-red realm. In Wyoming,

Time-compressed bones can oxidize
With one breath of fresh air and literally
Vanish. Trexler, the paleontologist, wraps

Each stony find in a plaster cast, to remove
It to the lab. Cocooned, perhaps, for years,
The relics await a fine chisel's tapping

That will map surfaces of vertebra, tibia,
Pelvis, or skull. Sometimes teeth marks
Reveal a territory battle millenniums old.

My father wanted pumice from Iceland.
The 1958 Encyclopædia Britannica
Proclaimed the powder a natural island

Product. To fulfill one request in a lifetime
Of few expressions, I roamed
Every chemist shop

For black magic in a jar, and found
Only a chunk of porous, volcanic
Rock stolen from a black sand beach,

Which I carried to drop into my father's hand.
I told him that they must not make
It nowadays. "Not making any more rocks?"

He laughed. Five months later,
The pocked stone sat in my living room.
We buried him next to his mother.

LARAMIE, OR OUR TOWN

Outside of Laramie,
Matthew Shepard was hitched to a post
And beaten. He had a sweet

Disposition, which saved him
No trouble and spared
Him nothing, not even

His life. Two rowdies thought
They'd get away with murder
By pointing the finger.

I stretch my legs around quiet blocks,
Through a neighborhood where
Children roam freely home

From school. In the next generation,
In the dead night of any town,
Will the owl hoot a different cry

And the moon look down
On a world gone to sleep
And finally awakened?

IMMANENT CREATION

Standing over the graves of Vincent
And his brother, I felt a vague stirring, as of
A journey commencing from Auvers-sur-Oise.

I then walked the surround of yellow fields
Brushstrokes have illumined. Art takes a life-
Time, gathers from the living, yet returns

Far more than reflection. There may be
No other way than this to live, risking
Nothingness. In the background, in the corner

Of a rustic bedroom draped in blue, inside
A sound, within a color transformed by
Lucidity and the sheen of varnish,

What is it that you can see?

WHEN LEAVING NO RE-ENTRY PERMITTED

Un billet, a ticket, marked no return.
Here wander, inhaling scents of lush
Pink blooms. Drooping and dripping

From quick snips, invisible trusses.
It is almost too much, this plot snug
As a suburban yard, a verdurous

Palette. Wander trodden paths,
Heady with deep cultivation. The pace
Sweeps along to the ponds. Don't glance

Back to the charming abode. Each
Leather chair bears the impression
Of a wide, famous behind,

The impression that this painter
Has just stepped out for an extra loaf
Or a plein air sketch.

Alas, without proper credentials,
Claude Monet cannot rejoin us:
Toute sortie du Musée est définitive.

LAST EXPOSURES

After more than a year,
My mother hands me his camera
Straight from its case.

I move outside to photograph
The paint job, drips and daubs
Left by a sloppy hand,

Evidence of the widow's lot:
Targeted for shoddy work.
Even her car wheel was ripped off.

I shoot the remaining three frames,
Go back inside to rewind,
Reload. The canister plops

Into my hand, his last exposures.
I try to imagine them
At the far end of the banal—

Whales blowing breath from the depths,
Molten whorls inside the moon—
Afraid to see what he's left us.

HOME MOVIES

From the basement, a mold-crusted
Projector and ten metal
Canisters emerge. Silent home movies

Shot when more light was required,
And the memories we made had to take place
In the open on sunny days.

We remember the beach, the bent
Serving spoon scooping sand,
Glinting now its natural silver,

Better preserved than flesh that flickers
Black and white, assuming a gray
Tone of regret. Three minutes of little girls

Dancing in tutus across the lawn.
Then a clip of soldiers on leave, sporting leis,
Hawaiian shirts. They stand facing

The photographer, not opening
Their mouths or moving. This is not
A still, but it's hard to tell the difference.

"Where is that?" we ask over and over.
And not recognizing our father, "Who are
Those men?" The refrain repeats without our

Comprehension. "That was the war.
Now, it's bedtime." We leave our father
Flicking ashes in a darkened room.

A FRAGMENT OF THE AUTHOR'S MANUSCRIPT IN HER OWN HAND, II

In the final circle, at the end of Hell,
Dante climbed the hairy left leg
Of the old monster himself,

Against gravity, lost in the short locks
Of the torso, disoriented as the master
Botticelli must have been—

Fifteen years (1480-95) he pored over
Sheep's vellum with metal stylus
Gripped, then inked those grooves,

Making visible delicate circle and year.
Hell wore thin as the master's
Hair, though more detailed than Paradise,

Which piddled out in a splash of light.
Blank pages torn from a hidden book—
No one bad and no one good.

FIVE MINUTE EXPOSURE, LARGE FORMAT

The moon comes up like an almond
And down like an orange.
It wasn't the moon, but the mountain.

The moonfish has a face that ends
In a healing. Your hands pass
Over the gash and all at once

There is singing. At thirty-five,
I was laid out by an ex-communicated priest.
His hands felt like a firewalk

On a hot afternoon. The priest
Was a drunkard, but what did it matter?
The face of the moonfish

Slashes through the sky. The clouds open,
The light dances, angling in from the playa.
No one knows where the shadows

Come from. It's a mystery, like the hands
Of the priest, like the almonds that slip
From the blood orange of the night.

When his hands touched my forehead
I fell to the floor. I had asked to feel
What my lover felt, she who was

Opened by a surgeon's knife,
By the touch of a rapist when only
A child. Why should I feel what she

Wished to forget? I asked to know empathy.
I fell into a swoon and landed curled
On the floor. When she woke

From anesthesia, I gently stroked her
Forehead. The first words she spoke
Were "No, please don't."

TWENTY MINUTE EXPOSURE

The risen mountain, a block of polished iron.
Think of an iron after the fire is gone,
Its pyramid cooling on the silver

Board. What it meant to be a woman, a wife,
I watched my mother to learn. What I
Was taught: iron the underwear, after sprinkling

It from a bottle. Iron the handkerchiefs.
This is the article I was taught first to iron,
Not a shirt. With handkerchiefs, a little girl's

Mistakes don't matter. The square is folded
And placed in your father's back pocket.
Why do men use only cloth to blow

And women use paper? What I learned:
The invisible work of women, the wrinkles
On their faces. I learned that women can spend

Their lives making the world a better place for men.

ONLY THYME

I pull you out by the roots, fierce love,
But you still smell of thyme and lemon.
What were you thinking, to die

Instead of wintering, after so many seasons
Of spring shoots and new greening?
Surely your gnarled, woody fibers

Are more alive than they look.
Yet after patient weeks of rain, nothing
Grows except the cutting I potted,

A woolly patch dwarfed by purple basil.
Making space for new plants, I pull up
Withered stems, baring your roots, and

The scent runs through me, like music
Pouring through a sieve
Of consciousness, leaving only this.

KENNEWICK MAN

Someone found Kennewick Man
Washed up on the shore—
9,000 years of bones.

Bury him or study him—
Two cultures in one can't decide
What needs to be done.

He might be Polynesian
Not Asian as continental drift suggests.
Either way, the tribes say he belongs.

A white man was found in his house
After only two years. Neighbors
Said he wasn't a friendly guy,

And one day he just disappeared,
Stepped inside from the porch
And dropped dead in his easy chair.

His house was sold for taxes owed.
Neighbors said that no one missed him.
Indians claim their Kennewick man.

GHOST FAMILY

A big welcome to the Ghost Family Reunion.
We only meet at funerals
In Holiday Inns south of the Mason-Dixon.

In little-used backwaters,
We blend into the scenic Blue Ridge Mountains
Or follow our progeny to the Atlantic

As if we were a river winding to the coast.
But we are only a few sad reminders
Of the legions on the other side of the line:

Your sister, your husband, your aunt,
Uncle, cousin, mother, your father,
Your brother, your youngest child.

It's just a bad dream when we wake in cold,
Air-conditioned rooms, but our fashions
Confirm it: black stockings and black lapels,

Matched boutonnière, a touch of black humor.
If only this were prom night
And not a dance macabre.

With so many gone now, it's a shock
To have one more burial to attend.
It's like our own service after a while—

We start taking issue with the hymns,
Choosing our favorites, humming them
Instead. We want a jazz funeral, but then

We stop ourselves to wonder if we're still
Alive and kicking. And if we are not, what
Would it take to raise us from the dead?

And if we are still breathing,
What would it take to make us feel something
More than sad? Line us up and shoot

Our formal portrait. We're the Ghost Family
Reunion, the short living in front,
All the dead towering over us to the rear.

PEPPER, 1930

A dark puckering means over the hill, off
The vine, misbegotten of time,
Forgotten.

That I am singing in the dark
For direction. That I am locked
In the dark heart of an Edward Weston

Photograph of a green garden pepper,
Nothing exotic. And yet not even
The pepper itself can guard its sensual

Thoughts. They range, reveal, conceal.
When I buy a pepper
I rinse it under tap water. I sometimes

Tap it for steam, scraping
Out the white seeds
As if I could purify us both

And suspend what might happen.
Then I wash my hands, collapse
In a heap, fall down and worship

All nature wrapped in thin green skin, the slick
Curve of an expressionless face,
Everything and everyone who has carried

Us to this place.

ON ATHENA'S SHOULDER

The owl's cat eyes echoed the high beams
and I swerved. I knew nothing more.
It must have lighted on the country road
sometime before. I took the last curve

and dipped down a slope
where I had once spun on ice,
end over beginning, like a planet
toppled in the tilt of seasons.

Hearing, still, the voices of the evening
and my own erratic wisdom
looping my inner ear, I almost missed
the horned owl swiveling to confront me

with its white throat. All of the words
in my head turned, then, into owls.
At the center of every question hunched
a silent owl, a silent way of knowing.

And I was left wondering
whether field mouse or broken wing
had downed it there, wondering who
would come along and hit it square.

DANCERS AT THE EDGE

I've grown used to the ones
who wander close, brave
with velvet antlers, who sneak up
when I'm raking leaves,
reading, or planting bulbs.
We eye each other, theirs
darker, more reflective
than mine. These creatures,
wild and new to this world,
do not flinch at human
scent. I will teach them
distance, prepare them for
November guns. I clap
my hands, bang plastic pots
and wait for them to run.

Two dancers entwine tawny necks,
bow to taste wild mushrooms.
The poison is all in my head.

INDIAN PIPE

Thinking "mushroom," I plucked the ghost plant's
Pale, umbilical stems before its bowed,
Translucent heads could bloom. No herbalist
Would have confused the two, or doubted

The potency of this juice for stinging
Eyes and root for sleep. Indian pipe grows
Infrequently on wooded slopes where slow
Changes can take hold without our knowing

And wildflowers can be colorless, odd
Albinos, rare as *agape* in a world
Of eros. Where will we have to live,
The two of us, controlled only by love?

What leaf-strewn shade will nurture us until
Our scale-like leaves unfurl, longings fulfill?

RESEMBLANCES

A delta, tributaries
seen from above,
branches like the roots of a tree.

The white mask of a cow's face,
like bones beneath
bleached free of any fleshly trace.

Sea urchins release white sperm,
smear eggs like stars
into a spiral galaxy.

Fractals endlessly repeat
the whole in parts
only unfocused eyes can meet.

Nature favors likenesses,
mirroring you
and me, our puzzling kisses.

LUNA

Sliding open the doorway to my house,
I let in lime-green moon moth's pendulous
Wings that wax and wane in tremulous swings
From ceiling to floor. I douse fast the lights
Inside and flick the floods, hoping Luna
Will flutter to glass, hang there, wait. Dusted
Wings are fragile things and touching them means
Uncertainties, effects of life or death
Wrought by pure desires to help nature
Become nature, to keep ambiguous
Boundaries clear from creature to creature.
Luna flies out, and I exhale, then catch
A breath: she flings herself back through the slot
Into my hands of longing and release.

On the summer solstice, sated from touch,
I wake to my cyclical blood and ache.
As I wipe away the signs, I hear
Rattling heartbeats of Luna's wings against
The bathroom screen, as if in a battle
Of wills with me, strangely attracted yet
Free.

A VARIATION ON "THE ROSES OF SAADI"

This morning I wanted to bring you roses
but the tight knot in my throat
was like a belt cinched close
around my dress, my dress covered with roses.

This morning I wanted to bring you roses
but the knot burst, I said your name,
and petals flew in the wind to follow waves,
painting them red with flame.

Tonight my dress carries your scent,
a fragrant souvenir. I breathe in
roses, think the knot in my chest might erupt
like the bud time could not restrain.

IN THE BELLY

Earrings, like a pair of wedding gloves:

a young clerk in the old world sells me white stones
from the window display. *Amber*, she intones,

and repeats, *amber*. Neither luminescent
fault-spiked caramel nor silent,

opaque coffee grounds, these crisp stars in night
sky draw my eye, my sight

slightly marbled by desire. I'm pondering another
I thought I'd lost like an old skin, a lover

set beside me in silver, to whom I was bound
and released, as from a watery deep brown.

I've climbed to err on autumn earth upon a crust
of papery leaves and spoken what I must,

yet conversations never end
when words wound inside begin

to surface through agents
like developing prints,

the way history seeps into the present hour
with purposes and meanings long turned sour.

A photograph appears darkest, tree
limbs serrating sky, where the negative is nearly

transparent. Chaos moves into form
while rigid design breaks like a maelstrom.

Beneath cathedrals, bridges, each grand structure
lies the grave of a worker,

a reversal. Where the world is torn
like a ticket, in the garden of betrayal worn

raw, I find the oldest amber
grown white and remember

the scars in the belly of love.

SANDSTORM

We were only teenagers in pup tents
Pitched on the outskirts of Zion,
Utah, along the Virgin River.

In 1974, we thought the war was over.
The summer night wrapped us
In its blaze, our gang lapped up
With one extravagant astral gesture.
Back east, never had we gazed
Into enlivened sky as fierce with stolen fire.

Our Promethean dreams came heavy-laden
As sacks of stone. Uneven ground
Beneath our thin foam beds
Brought ambiguous rest,
As we rolled to the Pacific west
In an old school bus painted blue.

Something rose up from the south
That night in Zion and gut-punched
Us while we slept or didn't. Over the border,
In Uzbekistan or Turkmenistan, exported sand-
Storms like these are known as "Afghans."

A force more fierce than wind alone
Sucked our structure of fragile aluminum
Until the forms, the dimensional spaces
Of our breathing, collapsed,
And we slashed through any opening, gasping.

>

The sky turned its back and tumbled
Into our mouths like blackened ash.
Arms outstretched, we tried our faulty reason
On the distance and the darkness
And the irrational, raging wind.

With all the lights stripped
From the back of the sky, we tied our souvenir
T-shirts into face turbans to sift oxygen

From the sand that emblazoned our skin.
We walked blind, battered by haze,
Until our eyes stung, rid of illusions, until
Every one of our prayers had been undone
By the wilderness we had wanted to know.

We were just teenagers in pup tents,
Intent on experience, and *oh brother, goddamn,*
How it would find us, again and again, wherever we hid.

POEM FOR THE PARDONED

From hypoblast to this acknowledgment:
no one knows why

the strange just keep on breathing. I
am wondering about the pardoned

and the condemned, one Sunday afternoon,
peering through the pollen-smeared windows

of my glass house in the woods. After winter
queries and postcards bearing quips,

Just be somewhere, I tell myself.
Even in a cell,

behind bars, there's a sense of belonging.
I know that

every kiss burns a question mark into the skin's
recall. I know that

every birdsong I hear can't be serious.
I think I'll answer as my dying aunt once did,

if anyone asks,
"What have you been doing?"

I've been being, she said.
I laughed,

hurrying out the door to a film.
Now I see her perfection.

BUDDHA GOING OUT OF BUSINESS

Buddha balances in the backseat
of the jeep, shoulder-harnessed,
and for good measure,
child-proof locked. I drive through
the bank, make a deposit.

Buddha cost twenty-one dollars
plus odd change. Not much
for a plaster-cast, bronze-painted
incarnation. I waited a week
for the final mark-down,

worried that I'd miscalculate
this moment. But now I'm happy,
so happy, with my Buddha.
I drive through for burgers,
one with cheese, one without.

I curb my Buddha, chew burgers because
my last lover eschewed meat and lied.
Alone with my balancing,
balancing Buddha, I think:
This is the best of lives.

NATURAL WONDER

A three-eyed calf
not golden idol
but emblem of this world
curled within world,
the naturally estranged.
News of its birth
in morning print, *Truth*
Stranger Than Fiction
next to the week's weather
in brief. The graven
image photographed
by the farmer's boy
who wants to be a vet,
who twisted the calf
to life. They won't kill it
yet, might be worth cash.

THE JUST NORMAL

Circus concerns, but
what of us, the *just* normal,
with candy-apple trials
and monsters of love?

What of that summer Daddy broke
a set of soap-box bonus
dishes on the hot barbecue?

Then Mother tried to immolate
autumn with paper-bagged cinders.

The sideshow competition
of siblings at 306:
I rang loudest when the china shattered
& saw the smoke rise first.

Memory:
a bat wriggled an eye-sized hole,
passed through the gnat screen, settled
in the artist's hair (my sister's)
with turpentine scent. She whooped,
we came running, but the canvas
was spoiled by the struggle
(*Leda and The Swan*).

AMERICAN BEAUTY

Arise and follow   this Christ said
Let the dead   *bury the dead.*

A stalk on the garden wall   out
of window-sight. Shear the dross
swollen Beauty's blossom
one night   dark   and seldom thought
one not quite
as poets predicted.

Yet I will snip for you
                     a red keepsake
a dash of petals clean as a razor slash
in an alabaster bowl.

Floating Ophelia recollects,
'twas Beauty killed the Beast.

APPARENT MIRACLE

Wonder in gnarled wire, a rabbit
snared, rent miraculously free,
unharmed. Riffling the winter husk
of field, white-tailed, it follows
scent to Fairy Land, a place
we named as children. Bluebells
sprouted either side its entrance,
a crawl tunnel thatched of sticks
and forsythia grown to ground.
This rabbit warren, moss crusted, lush
with bearing dirt, no light slatted
for shrubs, just Jack-in-the-pulpit,
a score of wind flowers, untouched,
and trees bowing branches to brush
the green mat. On bare knees
we hushed under weeping cherry buds,
pretending our warren was a house
we would never outgrow.
Without our making up rules,
something there made us whisper
thank-you prayers.

MAGDALEN DEER PARK, OXFORD, 1979

Let's trek around the deer park   with cameras in hand
outside the brilliant blue   a fence composes
breezes blow intermittent   a magnified symmetry
of vertical/vertical/of vertical   sisters look through
see deer   across a narrow stream   few words pass
between the two   and in this stream
float clots   that are not   ducks
and in the brush   hush   one is thinking of rabbits

Doe and green-horned buck   a movie with moving parts
we move around   seeing in spectroscopic flashes
the center spinning whole   on a misted day
of photographs   of slides   and stings of color

Snap the shutter   as an animal dances close
lens and slanted mirror   slipshod seconds   we study
later   our flat past   to remember
hypnotized   we flip pictures   lost in a deer's dark pupil
upside down in the eyes of the other   we steal
portraits in hats   taking turns
morphic resonance   this replication between sisters
exchanging scant memories   blurred velvet antlers

SNOW ROSE

At first, I thought
a huntsman cut out my heart,
but when I learned
he excised the boar's heart
instead, I cried for the beast
lost, knowing the heart's truth
still meant death.

Always Rose Red, youngest daughter
in another story (to distinguish
myself from sister's Snow White),
the kind Beast awaited my loyalty—
while she, her Prince's kiss.

I promised to be the Beast's wife,
he turned to Prince.
Sister's Prince woke her—
off she rode, ever after
that better-kept castle life.

VANISHING LADY

That look of horror spoils your lovely face.
What if it should show even through the wax?
                —Henry Jarrod in *House of Wax* (1953)

Phoenix illusion: a woman sinks
in projected flames to ash
placed in an ornate urn,
for incantations to return
her fated life in prestidigitation.

A common misconception: that James I
condoned the execution of witches
at stake. Others, perhaps, were burned—
murderous slaves, wives who performed
mayhem or poison upon their mates
or decided to take the lives of children
after a fashionable wait.

Carl Hertz, Illusionist
(indigenous dry goods clerk),
swore his first Vanishing Lady
to secrecy of craft, sealing the pact
with the wax of marriage. Mrs. Hertz
(née D'Alton) disappeared daily
in a *ménage à trois* of mirrors.
Sometimes, as Spirit Wife,
she appeared to float
just below her husband's hands, horizontally
rising over vocal objections—
out of sight, she didn't much mind.   >

George Méliès' *Vanishing Lady* (1896),
a dance macabre instead of conjured space,
but that was just (instinct) a camera trick.

Joan of Arc heard voices of dead saints
(Catherine, Michael, and Margaret, I think).
Pray tell, what crossed her up?

FANTASMAGORIE

Of his magic lantern's last image ciphered on smoke,
Robertson exclaimed (Paris, 1794),
"The fate that awaits us all."

After the spectres of flesh writhed cool, the screen
of chemical dust dispersed, what should emerge
but Mr. Bones jangling in the works
(like peacocks splayed by cogged gears,
or self-impelled windmills
taking turns in still interiors).

                    The dance macabre
played its gig, a slick soft-shoe, tap interlude,
a clogging reel. Grown gentlemen gasped, ladies collapsed,
agog before such thanatopic optics.

DID THE SOULS GO

Into history, or did they go forward in time? I thought I saw them marching right beside me in the band. I thought they might be tuba players, so much like me that they were almost disregarded, save for timely toots. Then I learned they never lied to save their skins. And saw the husk as problematic. They without it, free, and I enmeshed like a Halloween costume built of flimsy chicken wire and paper so neither part could stand alone. Souls were free to tell the truth about famine, poverty, greed, and the like. Then I saw how the truth must suffer, ideas shot down in our stead. I know ideas can die like us, and be born, bolstered, defended, forwarded, quashed, revised, short-sighted, warped, far-reaching, outmoded, cyclical, impractical, matter-of-fact, romantic, repressed, bright, based on false information. Sometimes the embodiment of an idea gives it too much weight and nothing constructive to do.

GREAT BLUE

It's no accident that I see you in the rushes and think of baby Moses, the one Bible story I really remember. I identified with that baby, if not with his future. I knew what it was to float, abandoned, in a rigged basket. I knew what it was to sleep through rills and undercurrents with someone always claiming good intentions. But enough of me, that's all in the past. Now, it's you, Great Blue, who holds my attention, on hinged spires, fishing the icy creek. You were gone all summer. I know because I was here. Where on earth were you, bird? It got boring and strange without you, though today I only think of you when I see you. When I never saw you, I thought about you constantly. Or maybe I was thinking about me, so, well, blue here without you. Why can't I even look at you without thinking about myself? I'd rather try being you, just for the second or two when you balance over the water and swallow something real.

IRRELEVANT VIOLET

Velvet purple petals like the darkened room where he is tugging his
pajama top after brain surgery and claiming to be someone he is not.
I cannot stop the violent thrashing of one thing into another—I used
to call it metaphor—when parents become children, the quick
transformative leaps that strand one in a farther country with
knowledge only of irrelevant words, an arm that used to bend that
now hangs limp, *love,* a notch carved at the site of recurrence. The
body is a geography in which all countries float. I start with the
surface because that is what I think I know. Beneath this shallowness
nothing is certain. Skin changes its tension and texture. Sometimes
we all forget our manners, especially when we are in pain. Sometimes
as I am loving someone they leave and return with a scar in a place
that falls beneath my hand. Nothing can predict a seamless surface. I
want to save a room for you. I want to know that the you I know will
always be there.

SELF-REFLECTION

In this poem, I promise, you will learn everything I know about myself. Despite the fact I get it wrong, I've been looking in the mirror my whole life. I think I see myself, but as you know from your own experience, that's rarely the case. How ridiculous that we spend so long gazing at the unattainable, fooling ourselves with our own faulty facts, our faces flying toward us exactly backwards. We could spend that time dancing or reading out loud. We could make love more often and try to keep our minds from wandering. After all these years I can't even pick myself out in the class photograph. But I can recognize your face anywhere. It could be that, actually, objectivity is underrated and love its greatest example. This relegates relativity to twentieth century egotism, nothing more than a medieval scheme to place the earth at the center once again. Just a theory. And there are others. For example, I have believed that growing a good tomato is as important as writing a poem. For example, I have believed in the open exchange of ideas. I have believed we are not the same and this is the greatest liberation.

TEXAS SCHOOL BOOK DEPOSITORY

You walk the labyrinthine Louvre, not looking for the mystical grin forbidden to photographs. You are walking instead to the end of galleries that never end only turn. You cross hallways, traverse staircases to similar galleries, following the rectangles on the walls through mythological and biblical subjects, searching for something you are not certain how to recognize, something known only by what it is not. And it is not the bullet buried in Connally's thigh, that stubborn meteor clue buried with Connally when he died. The images every room holds ricochet off your eyes to meet where benches, were this America, would offer rest to tired, swelling feet. In Europe no one sits to view art, and everyone pays to pee. One must keep moving along through the centuries, so many of them, centuries in Europe, especially in formerly Eastern Block Europe, where most gallery guards, too many of them, have not yet adjusted to the crumbled wall. There, it is still possible to be observed breathing too heavily on the art. Remember the Swiss woman in Prague, missing parts of several fingers, who accosted you in hard-edged, French-accented English. "Beal Cleenton, sex-u-al-ity," she kept repeating. She'd heard something on TV. One of her many rings fell onto the breakfast table. You found the ruby near the butter and gave it back, astounding her with your Honest Abe. By twists and false turns, startled middles and ends, you head toward something lost. It is not the date, November 22, 1963. You remember just where you were, on the sidewalk in front of your house, excited because the buses brought friends home early from school. Too large, containing everything, the Louvre is no place in which to be addled or alone.

149

You make a decision to find your way back to Egyptian Antiquities. There, in a profusion of detail, you are able to focus on a small vial whose purpose remains unclear. A little-known fact: our dead President's brain has vanished—no one knows where.

BABY

Pink and puffy, dragged by the ear. As it flew into the air, I saw the life-sized doll was no real baby, thank God. I added it to the list of toys my dog had found in the woods. My dog is fond of plastic in any form. I was the one who thought the severed hand with the dog bone in the palm was a cute chew toy. I had to encourage him at first, especially at parties. I know the meaning of what goes around comes around. The doll baby hit the ground. In a few short weeks he had dissected the baby. An arm here, a leg abandoned over there, until only the moldy torso and head, semi-attached, were left. The day I came home to find him tossing the head into the air I barred him from the rest. But it was too late. He'd buried the other pieces and would dig them up at the worst possible moments. He presented me with a well-chewed arm and cowered as I burst into tears. The week my divorce was final he brought me the head again, wagging his tail. I thought I'd taken that dreaming expression to the dump along with the well-teethed torso. I didn't know what to do. I picked up the head. When its impossibly blue eyes opened, I threw it and said, "Fetch."

THINKING TO SCALE

In New York harbor, renovated Ms. Liberty waits after dark. From the shore she looks unimposing to me, though her illumination's pretty. I've always envied my sister's coming of age in the sixties, because she could scale the narrow stairs and look down from the precarious arm. Contemporary tourists are left only the view from the crown. In the Seine, a model Liberty oversees the Bateaux Mouches tours. The boat rounded her while all around me jolly Italians, Germans, and Japanese snapped. In Luxembourg Gardens I found her again and posed warily, before an even more shrunken replica, for a young woman on Golden Week tour who insisted we exchange the favor. While I waited for elevators at the Eiffel Tower, every language echoed awe laced with dread. Down below I thought I saw her, a speck among specks. I could not be sure. I looked for Liberty again in Prague, presuming that she followed me. On the hill opposite Hradcany, where the castle by night appears swathed in otherworldly light, I found a model of the Eiffel Tower. It is nearly impossible to believe in where we live, for at any moment it is possible to uncover places from which we came, pale models of our larger, freer selves. Plato had some good Ideas.

CIVIL RIGHTS

It was always the riots they showed on TV. "We shall overcome," far in the background. I lived in a small southern town where Blacks were rare items. Some of the only ones I ever saw up to the age of ten were burning down the city they lived in. I wanted to be a good little girl. Disorder worried me: demonstrations, sudden thunder, pictures of mud-crusted soldiers, going to sleep without pushing in all the dresser drawers and lining up my shoes, nuclear holocaust, my father's intermittent fits. It wasn't until sometime in the seventies when I, in a mini skirt, voted with the majority (against my father's wishes) to integrate our church that I understood my mother's standard reply to the question of how she'd voted in any election: "It's a secret ballot."

RED BEETS, STEAMING

Only the small ones cook through. The large ones take a long time; they're tough and never cry. They've held it together through thick and thin. It's hard to love them, but once you see them soften—if you're willing to wait it out—these tough old beets now tender thank you sweetly. Everything worth waiting for has to take so long, has to have so much longing in it. I heard a man say that for a year and a half he had been in a dark place. I wonder what deep tenderness was struggling to come out. His hair turned white, waiting. Beets come from dark places, too, and after they cook the water's blood red, not pretty pink like ribbons on a girl's silky head, or borsch in a plain white bowl, but rougher, richer, as if you didn't wash them thoroughly enough. I want to return to that darkness where the root took hold—of beginnings without ends—and there's nothing to say.

GOD ATTACK

The girl floats down the country road—oh how the glorious cows
and pretty horses roam and graze. The girl wanders past,
daydreaming in the pastoral setting, the icing on the cake she's eating
every day. She's thinking about the nature of God, but the message
traveling through the air converts, and, lo, dogs come instead to eat
her. On the horizon they gather and growl and run to set upon the
girl and wrestle her to the ground leaving blood, embedded gravel,
nightmares, and later scars. All thoughts of nature being God go by
the way. All nature gods turn ugly to her sight, and surely are not
God, not the one she had in mind when the dogs came out of the
blue, charging through goldenrod, which if she considers her allergies
should have been a sign. She realizes with embarrassment that she
wants to limit God in this small way (and that others want to limit
God in other ways) and that to limit God at all is just the opposite of
what she had in mind when she was wandering down the road,
expanding. All in all, she's glad that she was only set upon by dogs.
And thanks be to whatever.

READING SIMONE WEIL AT A TENDER AGE

"We love like cannibals," she wrote, at an early age, this Jewish Christian, who never converted, who refused to eat at the age of four when she learned French soldiers didn't have enough food. These are facts I remember of her. Here are some facts about me: I locked my bedroom door and read behind it during adolescence. One time my father kicked my poodle. Only words held my attention. Right after he screamed something incomprehensible about everyone being out to get him and slammed his fist into a door, my mother used to say, "Your father loves you in his own way."

BABY, IT'S COLD OUTSIDE

This will be your only notification that I am not in charge of your life. I would say this announcement comes from "a friend," but of course you know better. Don't let it get to you. After all, I'm only a disembodied figment of the universal urge for absolutes. To paraphrase you on a generous day, God is, at best, an internalized *I am*. To get in touch with me all you need is therapy, years of it perhaps, but with your salary I'd say the money will be less difficult than finding the time. Have a nice life. But first, a bit of advice: The middle of the road is no safe haven. The turtle got stopped halfway by a pickup that left arched claws clutching pavement and a long neck straining from a crushed shell. There are plenty of other warning signs, but I doubt you've missed them. I've noticed that you try to wish them away, employ logic at the very moment of insight. Just an observation. That's what I'm here for, remember. I am the observer, and you, well, you are in a position to be observed, which just about sums up our relationship if you ask me. But I've noticed that you rarely do. So, I'm giving you my notice, not that I expect you to acknowledge the change. In *Neptune's Daughter* (1949), two couples sing comic duets in consideration of attraction and bad weather. Ester Williams sings, "I really must go." Ricardo Montalbán begs her to stay. The other couple mirrors this arrangement: Betty Garrett wants to stay and Red Skelton would rather she go home. In each case someone's wishes take precedence. It happens in belief, too, and in knowledge. One has to take a stand and change in order to move. True, there's balance in all things, but remember I am the fulcrum, not you.

RENOVATION

It's no secret that Napoleon coveted Prague as his Seat, no matter
that his obsession with symmetry, great vistas, and straight, spoking
streets would have left him trembling in twisted alcoves afraid to
sleep. No secret that Hitler imagined himself at the end of the war
ensconced in Prague castle, his bunker on the hill. And now it is
young Americans seeking refuge for ideals, while natives who poured
out over the years stay west, away from the anxiety of history. As a
resident of the only defeated country in America, I understand ex-
patriot Czech fear, how it must feel to live on two sides at once, with
someone outside always placing you somewhere because of how you
sound. On my last morning Mrs. Kubešová finally asks me her
question. She has drawn two continents, a dollar sign, wings and
arrows that have brought me here. My bags packed heavy for
traveling, I write the answer on her pad. The day before, I paid her in
sturdy marks for her foreign account, obliged to pass my dollars
through inconvertible Czech crowns. She writes beside my number a
question, "U.S.?" I nod. Her eyes calculate and darken. In my next
series of gestures punctuated by spare words from the Czech/English
dictionary we share, I invite her to visit America. For two people
present to each other, lack of words means nothing. But the flight on
the airplane she has drawn would take all the money she could save in
six years. "America," she says and throws her arms wide. " Český," she
says softly and holds her finger close to her thumb.

MONT SAINTE-VICTOIRE OF THE LOCAL

My Mont Sainte-Victoire stares through the windows with the moon. Cézanne's rose green into the afternoon. My mountain follows me like a shadow. Cézanne's could be studied like a field of cattle. And when I drive the dark road home, thick white faces shine from fenced edges. Cézanne sat straight in the saddle, bootheels settled in the stirrups like wedges. I am never alone: the many phases of the moon surround me, feed me, clothe me, see me, see me. As if I were a tulip bulb planted exactly six inches, awaiting my cue. As if you, Cézanne, were here in my house, sipping light-colored Kenyan coffee, standing at my window, staring toward my mountain, holding a hand-painted china cup and saucer of my coffee. My lover stands quietly at the sliding door, holding a tiny pine tree covered with Christmas packages. Because he has walked with it through the cold and chosen to stand and watch me through the glass before knocking, the needles will fall, the tree wither. All of this a memory, hardly real. My mind is aching with memories as Cézanne stands at my window, staring toward my mountain.

JACKIE IS DEAD

Mrs. Kubešová shows me a Czech headline, and as she points, she says, "Jackie, Jackie," in the universal language of celebrity. We are sad for a long moment, staring together at a photograph that takes us back to the sixties, I to a small Southern town in America and my landlady to this very apartment, with its same arrangement of rooms opening into other rooms, its same fixtures, nothing missing but freedom. A young President lies shattered all over again. There's not much that can be said, especially between the two of us. Instead, we pass the newspaper back and forth and shake our heads. I can smell strudel from the narrow galley kitchen that I'm not allowed to use because of the intricacies of bottled gas and the stupidity of foreigners. No food except morning coffee is included with my room. I close the door to what was once the dining room and sit down to rest from my wandering. I've walked past the sixteenth-century Black Madonna, suspended in a cage attached to a cubist building. I've walked all the way across the Charles Bridge, as far as the house at Three Violins. In a few minutes, after a knock, Mrs. Kubešová sets before me a tray. I almost kiss her, but opt for a burst of applause. *"Dobry, dobry,"* I say between samples of apple strudel and tea. *"Dobry,"* she echoes, hovering as I eat. In this apartment near the end of a century, we exchange good for good.

THE EDITING ROOM

A room walks around,
two arms, two
legs, guarding the middle.

Anything can happen, has, in
a room.

An encounter scarred
the painted walls,
crumpled an antique chair
and an armoire like paper,
made one want
to renovate, begin again, in
a room:

a clear container
painted white,
an emptiness not of loss
but of space in which to move.
I say, *Nothing—this time—*
nothing will enter this
room
but from the bottom of the well,
dredged in a bucket
by my own strength.

Then you—
I remember *you.*
Uncertainty is the nature
of the room
where soft corners peak
to Mucha designs, sliced cabbages

or gynecoid blooms,
blending in a band of pink relief.

Everything begins, ends, in
a room.

This opening has been formally
established, like a cone,
a light source, or a shadow,
as conferring
a particular reality,
as of the father,
as of the mother,
as of myself,
first in a bedroom,
then an editing
room,

where I rolled the Moviola—
    when I thought I might burst—
forward and back, defying time—
    when you would not—
for a dark projection—
    when he donned the fedora—

where I kissed the sticky emulsion—
    when her body looped in Möbius confusion—
and I scraped, stripping layers of light,
    when my body excused my thought just long enough.

With darkness flaked over my hands,
I applied a thin line of liquid adhesive—
    when I was not myself and most myself—
in the editing room,
where the press of heat healed the split.

SWIMMING NAKED

Atlantic skinny-dipping
in the blue moon's full view,
sturdy Venuses yelp and stutter,
brave glistening foam
and old wives' tales of *Don't.*

Drunks stumble on the rocks
to dark river water, twist ankles
to a halt of shivering cold
and somersault beneath the surface
where night fish let gravity go.

Swim through night thoughts
that take away the breath.
Swim through family history
and the last gasp of bad luck.
Swim up, gulp water from a cup.

Some children arch while stroking,
faces awash with fear of loss.
Some learn to clip noses and seek
the slick pool's depth, sinking like
wishes, while mothers cry, "Come up."

THE VISIBLE WOMAN:
NOT A TOY BUT A LEARNING EXPERIENCE

That late sixties Christmas
after everyone's innocence had been shot away,
revealed as the pink pillbox
it had always been, she came
better than naked, completely unveiled,
internal parts made visible by a plastic shell.
Shapely in the hips and chest,
she looked the way I wanted to someday
(but not too soon). An unborn baby
fit perfectly beneath the removable dome
that could transform
her lean stomach.
                    I opened
the box and laid each organ, each bone, bare,
snapped and glued her into permanent 3-D, painted
kidneys, triangle bowels, liver, lungs, and
heart. Her blood turned the color I chose.
On impulse I painted the baby gray-blue,
to echo the veins in my arms.
Full-term, the baby would never be
born. The Visible Woman was not furnished
with a birth canal, nor could she speak to tell me
how she came to be *with child*. I was ten. I wanted
to know. It seemed to me then that I held power
over her. Most of the time I left the baby
floating apart from the woman, though
I remember snapping the dome onto her stomach
and pocketing the baby for myself,
indulging some dark, marsupial
fantasy of easy motherhood.
Or did her condition

finally explain the hushed tones
of *Immaculate Conception?*
My imperfect education left me vulnerable to
change. The women who taught me managed
to leave most of the inner story
out. I thought I worked like *her,*
with shell-like skin to hold in
what I needed, to keep away what I feared.
For years I did not believe
my skeleton held up my body
but thought the form depended on clear skin,
layers of carefully selected paint,
while the structure crumbled from within.

BURNED-OUT HOUSE

Daily, I drive past a burned-out house—
charred stone chimney,
cracked foundation—this boundary
of an old conversation, holding inside
wary stacks of blackened timbers.

Each time I cannot help
but look—in flickers, quick breaths—
piercing the hearth, to discern
more than facts, without risking
momentum or life.

My foot pushes harder on the gas
as I fix my gaze
on anonymous misfortune,
as if we might escape by going fast,
by way of empathy.

∞

Safe at home, I steady thoughts
by tramping. Footfalls are all
as autumn's light trips through

ocher orange, through red-rimmed leaves.
I descend the creek bank, alert
to hard echoes in the brittling woods.

Afraid and calm, I search
the sound's direction, walk on, filled
with water over thoughts, throat clotted,

until my eye meets a dark shape that heaves
its weight from a branch, that meets
another shape shuddering after its twin.

Repeating myself through fog
that twists around House Mountain,
driving toward you I pass shadows

hovered over something with a brush
of tail and vivid entrails stretched.
The turkey vultures' torque acts on red fox.

My slurring over gravel leaves them fixed.
Years take their toll, but reveal
love's skeleton after all we've said.

CONVERSATION, MOSTLY BLUE

after Matisse's Conversation, *1908-1912*

The conversation begins in the middle
Of the night
My wife in her dressing gown
I in pinstripe pajamas   smoking   my pipe

What we are discussing
When the green puff of tree
When the daubs of pink bloom
When the fire engine

When the gray strands I would never mention
Stray from behind my wife's ear
She leans back in her chair
Like a question

When my hands grip my flannel pockets
I know what we are discussing
Is over and
I am standing after the end   of what we know

LONG ROOTS

        steam from taut ground, pulse in your hands
as you tug the stump. Earth roils
and wakes, leaves memory troughs behind twin roots
that waver wild up to air.
What struggles dead things wield
to stay put where they lived:
You pull and pull and hear dull warnings
at your back, balancing
on ground long roots meander under. Pull
until your listening yields
damp echoes. When you are sure
the roots will not tame,
stop yanking. You will have to thwart them
with your blade, give up,
chop, leave something buried. The end
is where the heart is pumping, where you tend and mean
to go. You know the end
and the beginning. Your palms are stained,
hope-quickened. It is *now*
you least apprehend, and I
admit not even love knows what you have been thinking.

HINDQUARTERS, UNDER MOON

Three in the morning, the moon intent
on scorching the mountain raw,
and the dog is barking.
His din equals a million pots and pans
clanged for an eclipsed orb's return.
He's poised for action, nose pressed
to glass. The floodlight reveals
flocking deer, scattered ghosts,
too many legs in motion to count the number
of startled souls. Grazing acorns,
like contented cows, several don't budge.
Light severs one in a magic trick
that allows hindquarters
and a white plume supported by two legs
to construct a living creature.
I respect surrealism
in all of its forms.
I'm just sleepy enough
to observe macabre effects
under the unnatural moon. When the buck
tilts its gnarled, enormous rack
into the picture, completing itself
to bound away on pencil-point hooves,
I still can't believe what I see.

In Los Alamos I saw Fat Man's twin
suspended from the ceiling,
a metal moon over video screens
that left me sleepless.

My father fought in the Pacific Theater.
I once played the daughter who foresees
her village's Nazi conflagration

in *The Murder of Lidice.*
Kamikazes missed the deck of his flagship
by inches. As communications officer,
he received reports
that his fleet was dead.

The morning after the deer
my mother disturbs my sleep to tell me
the surgeon's prognosis.
The ridge in your father's head will sink
over time. He'll forget it's even there.
My father likes his doctor,
who recently served in the Persian Gulf.
After fifty years
this seasoned soldier
has opened my father's head
and relieved the pressure.

But that's not true. It's only been
six weeks since my father fell down
and whacked his head on the bed
in the middle of the night.
My mother said it sounded like
a bomb had exploded.

WOUNDED

The cat came to him unbidden, as all beauty must.
Staggering from an open sore, the animal
twisted to bite him when he reached down.
The cat had grown up this far knowing
that to be caught meant to be hurt.
A door slam had left only half a tail.
He wrapped the creature of bone and matted fur
to make it well with medicine from a dropper
and taught the cat by subtle measures
to trust him. The cat could stuff itself
until it felt full for the first time
in its life, eyeing him with bits of rich canned food
stuck on its greedy face.
Within a week the cat would take its medicine
without the confining towel.
After another, the cat mewed
when he came home, as if it missed his company.
He had given up on more, when the cat climbed
onto his lap, and he heard the purr
begin with an odd tremor, releasing
estrangement and injury and reproach
toward the strong and the well, a purr of finally
being held, uneven trust aired
in bursts of vibration almost like growls.
The cat purred through its buried scars beneath
lush-looking fur, purring from its loss
no matter how gently the man stroked the cat
and wanted to keep it always
safe inside his house.

BROKEN BUCKET

Bodies bloom in the surf
on this bright, reflective beach.
You've left me
not knowing what to think.
I tug my suit, gaze
through prescription shades,
and fault neither the patch of gauze
obscuring a woman's scar nor the thick
man's fur that flutters
in the breeze.
                    Dogs romp
through serious gulls. A boy
digs a hole with his one good arm
that finishes in a hand.
He cannot decide how to employ
the green plastic bucket
that won't hold sand.

UNDERWATER PHOTOGRAPH

What drives the force of love
if love drives us

to heights
and depths

submerging all the fears?
Submerging yourself, you learned

to search the darkness. Someone
who has stayed away from light

a long time can hold her breath,
can hold position, and strike

in a heartbeat. Beneath mask
and regulator, your face distorts,

a puffer fish I do not know I know.
For years we have swum side

by side, dodging native blood,
small-town hooks, and schools

that tried to teach us facts
better suited to your litigation

than my art, I thought.
I see that you have sought the depths

as eagerly as I, and found a way to open
your eyes in places other people

only see in photographs, tight frames
of liberation.

DOUBLE KARMA

Beneath this snowfall
Unhinging your arms like wings
An old crust of ice

Where the shovel clangs
You labor aching and numb
Shadowing the sun

AUTOPSY AFTER DEATH OF "LIGHTNING CONDUCTOR"

"Psychoses, usually of the maniacal type, have been
reported as occurring after lightning stroke."
   —*Ralph W. Webster, M.D., Ph.D.,* Legal Medicine and Toxicology (1930)

The ranger walked in the open to create
his persona. He waved his arms in false dawn
that beat on the lookout station
when spring came bearing storms.
No one witnessed the suffocation
behind his humorous tremor.

Seven times he staggered—veins singing,
vision blanked, bees' buzz diving his ear's whorl,
wounds of entry and exit, like stabs
in the hands and feet,
radiating red streaks coursing
Jupiter's bolt.

              We believe what we see:
the forest ranger's keys fused in his pocket,
a magnetized clump that will never unlock a door.
The charred band around his marriage finger.
Shadowed links leading to a disc
of heirloom time on his thigh.

If lightning follows the path of least
resistance, a man struck once, like a practiced
thief, will offer better conduction.
It is no wonder when a self-styled curiosity,
Believe It or Not, shoots himself one day
in his dark living room while the sun plays
down on the roof.

The coroner incises the decisive Y
in the chest of the man called the Human
Lightning Conductor, opens the shell
containing seven compressions
of wrath, dark as nightmare.

Lodged beside the left lung
between two crumbling,
cancerous bones,
the coroner locates
                          an obscure black stone,
theory's chance relic,
a perfect emitter of energies absorbed,
reflecting none. Lampblack's a common
example. Christ, another.

DOUBLE DROWNING

I can recall the movie
in Driver's Ed
of mannequin couples throwing their love
through windshields
because of what they were not wearing.

And in this vein, I remember
my Sr. Life Saving course that cold winter,
the license uncrimped in my wallet,
when I went to the YMCA after supper
to swim required distances.
I'd walk out into snowy nights,
my hair lightly frozen by the time I drove home
alone with an unexpected memory
stalking back
               of the horse who ripped a hole
bigger than three fists in his breast
and stood with a twitch of leather
gripping his muzzle
so he might forget the larger pain
while the vet cleaned his wound with a garden hose,
sending streams of startling color
into parched ground at my shoes. I could not look
away, I could not watch, I could not
say what I had come for, I could not forget.
Driving home, I saw the dark
circles flower into me
and stopped the car in time
to topple. The steering wheel stopped me.
I awakened, a dream later, weak, trembly,
and drifted toward home, through the door,
to hear my mother question,
"Did you get the job?"

"I didn't ask," I said
and saw her catch my expression as she turned
and saw her rush in slow motion, as if through water,
forever holding out her arms
for fear of my falling.
                    The final night
our teacher dressed in army boots, fatigues, and chains
and threw himself into the deepest part of the Olympic pool.
We were to save him any way we could, then pull
his weight one length before lifting his lungs to air.
It was worse than the warm-up test
when we jumped in carrying a mask
and snorkel, cleared the mask underwater, blew the last
of our breath out the snorkel
and continued to swim without our heads' surfacing.
It was worse than the cinder block.
But I forget exactly how that worked.

He flailed, looking more like he wanted to kill
than to sink. He pushed the buoyant objects
from him, lunged expertly toward my neck, interlocking
his fists. We went down six feet
while I only kept my head by thinking
what might happen if he ever let a student die like this.
I pushed his hips up, turned him, locked my arms, my fingers
barely meeting around the beef of his chest, rose
briefly, and rode him as if he were an octopus.
Spinning over and over, we inched toward the shallows.
Biting for air, holding on, held fast, pressing
an elbow into his heart, I kicked for all my life.

A vivid picture of double drowning lingers
in my mind
        the entwined couple in Russell's *Women in Love*
        hug against the drained pond's silt
        like fossils
of what might happen if one were to approach
a victim
without proper precaution.

      Better to let one drown than to
have entered the water
and bobbled down,
down to the waiting weeds of some green lake
or river bottom
or other,
down below day-
light, where no wind can stir the mirror
into shared circles of this perfect life.

DEAR FRIENDS

There is no such thing as perfect communication
as our train whistles north through fields
of broken pines that my eyes climb
branch after broken branch to their needled
widow's walks. I look out over this landscape,

panning through the movie it becomes,
and my mind wanders until I see, more
clearly than ever before, your
faces. Each window frames a changing composition,
sometimes my own face, that registers only as afterimage.

The conductor's voice sweeps the car.
Our cawing whistle stops as he tells us the time
has leapt ahead to Eastern Standard.
It's no surprise, for I have left
behind so many times, that only time, I fear,

can tell how long it will take
to come here again. Up ahead
the engine rounds a bend, almost knotting our train
into a circle, unfurling as we keep pace
on the track. If this motion should stop, my heart

would jump back, my head
balk, impatient to see the problem solved,
to be underway without the lingering whiplash
of memory. But it's not to be
so simple, friends.

We pass another stretch of calf-speckled green,
their white faces flash, while the boy sleeps on
his mother's breast, and the man who's lost his children
talks, and the girls who want
another Lucky step

into the aisle streaming cologne
that wakes some speculation.
I try not to stare too long at anyone,
but it's harder to stay aloof
than to touch

each seatback for balance as I rock along
this car into another and still others, finally
popping out onto the swaying platform
to look back
into the funnel of swirling color

where you wave, surely
moving your free hands back and forth in the air.
I can remember the ex-marine's story:
My boy's only twenty
but he looks like thirty. His mother stole

him and his brother from me years ago.
I got this photograph, no letter. You want to see
my tattoos? I looked at my boy's face and never felt
so sorry in my life. Look here, at this heart,
inside it says, "Glory."

THE ANGEL ON THE CEILING

After sex
you scratched a message across my shoulder
blades. (I thought back to that day
you drew the hexagram *Fu* up my spine—
five broken horizons
above a fine yang line.

I had to find its name, what it meant
in *The Book of Change,* before I could
answer you with truth, with what
you already knew—
yes, at the winter solstice
I would return to you.)

My first deciphering failed utterly.
I turned and faced up. A shadow
the clock made, a shot
of light through the lampshade.
I said *bat,* because I saw
a fixed, black bird.

You wrote the word,
index in air, and I thought
the shadow of wings edged
in a show of hovering:
                          your message
went unread upon the dark.

Angel, you said and pointed up.
I felt the word, distinct
on my skin, a repetition

mysteriously meant. By your gesture,
I saw on the ceiling a rare vision:
an angel, dark and still.

Until we turned the lamp
on, wings hovered there
and would return, invisibly with the light
above: the tangible unseen
of the shadow seen. Or an act of love,
turning in the dark to gesture all the time

toward what it is not, touching
to sense what cannot be touched.

WOMAN ONCE THOUGHT DEAD RECOVERING

*"I'm telling you, I've seen dead people 100 times in my life,
and she was dead. I saw a resurrection. I'm going to my grave
believing she had a second chance and this is a miracle."*
—Detective Gary Wright, Champaign, IL (AP)

I've been to one of those
places they told you about
where frozen blossoms go
to meet blizzards and float
coloring the snow.
Cold melts the petals,
sun melts the snow.
Where I go
no one comes after.
The stretcher stung my skin
when I woke
seeing the blade float
over my throat. I swallowed.
The coroner dropped his knife,
and I rose, wrapped up
in this sack of flesh, a woman
back from death,
the coldest spring.
See, my fingertips
so pink, like petals of water,
until you touch them white
to know my story.

A LADY WRITING A LETTER BY VERMEER

All day I am walking to the square
in the sun. I don't know what to say.
I've begun the letter but it lies
on a black tile in the sitting room.
It has been five years
since the child. There's no reason
for delay. I sip tea, plead
with the bargain-maker, sass
the servant-girl, but no luck.
I take a pinch of chocolate, search
birds' tracks at the corners
of my eyes. No one knocks.
So, what keeps me here?

It has taken this long to write.
Now, even you expect no reply.
That is as it should be.
I write to tell you I am alive.
What else is there? All the devils
you see in the air mean nothing—
this you know, so I write to assure you
you are not mistaken, your skin
is where you are not, around me
tight as stays. If I picture your face,
there is nothing left but this:
my stomach flowers as it once did.
I have not forgotten yet.

LADY READING A LETTER AT THE OPEN WINDOW BY VERMEER

A woman faces the light
which nearly always falls
left to right in Vermeer.
Its source is clear
as the window, as the cloudless day.
She slants the page to sun, her face a mask
except for a tiny dagger of dark
beneath her eye. Her ghost
reflects full-face from panes of glass.
What's in the letter?

Half a peach tilted from
the Delft bowl bears its seed
upright on the bed. The remaining fruit
struggles to mound, large green apple
pushing red and orange and plum,
while a few soft pieces spill,
the half-cut peach is one. The painter's
favorite chair fills the corner—
its left lion shadow now.
In this example, we can see
that the chair is emptier
than the woman's hands
as she stands to read what the sun
tries to erase:

To you I send my only letter.
This is all you will hear from me.
Each morning as I've painted you from memory
we have grown apart.
You must not see this picture.

It is unjust. I have tried to paint us
in painting only you. The face
that pretends to be yours on the glass
is mine as you read this letter.
If you were able to adjust
the green curtain to your liking
you would discover my usual
Cupid, bow in one hand—
this letter raised in the other.

IN FOCUS

Last night I tumbled out
in failing light, a day before
the year's autumnal equinox,
to see by headlights the way the road
unraveled past the tires' voice
and uneven heights of the outskirts'
built-up tangle. I headed south
by west, curved along the bypass
until the last exit that would shoot
me toward Pasolini's *Gospel
According to St. Matthew.*

But in a stranded field, left
holding green between interstate
and convention hotels, malls and airport,
industrial parks, a cloud had found
a way to wedge between straw and the falling
dark, so that a thick, white field
of drifting energy lay ghostly flat
to match the field's dimensions
and to mask its bitter, mathematical scars.

It brought in focus the dead
and the living—a groundhog eyed traffic
from the shoulder—so that I checked
the rearview mirror to echo
what there was to be seen
just beyond, as if through a pinhole:
I swerved to give the animal room,
forgetting the anger that forced
me, like a paper narcissus,
into blooms of speed, forgetting

my failings, forgetting that I drove alone.
I traced my dry lips with a fingertip,
unwilling to kiss away the hurt
in a show of love. The field was real,
almost too real to see, until you might
follow my gaze with your eyes that know.

FLIGHT LUCK

Apollo 13, can you hear us? This is Houston,
the future home of the Astros,
in the fisheye of mission control.
We are burning with reflections
on your three friends who were fired
in the multibillion-dollar kiln—one hell
of a spectacle. You see, this is Houston,
it was nonmetallic material that time,
in a pure environment
of oxygen, a tiny spark,
but we've fixed that now.
                              Galileo,
in 1610, invented a way to the moon;
he drew his own conclusions, sketched maria
in charcoal that still compares to photographs.
Sunspots incised twin stars
on the retinas of his eyes. The telescopic
limbs of light went out for him
one night.
            "Houston," we hear you calling,
"we've had a problem." But we thought
we had that solved, that's why we were dying
to defy the laws of luck, launch you charmed
at 1313 hours (someone's idea of a joke).
In just two days, it would occur
to us we might have made our second fatal
gaffe in much the same manner as our first.
This time, again, it was oxygen. A tank burst.
When we sent the ape, Ham, up, no one watched.
We never worried how to coach him down
to earth.
            Apollo crew, if you are orbiting,
reroute the poison gas, conserve water;

there are no lakes in space, alas. Eat light,
use your waste for ballast, and perhaps,
there's a chance, you will have enough
breath to see your flight back to us.
Good Luck.

LIGHTING THE DARK SIDE OF THE MOON

"We'll see you on the other side," beamed Lovell
before he saw for the first time
the far side of the moon.
                            Christmas Eve,
sixty miles out—for thirty-four minutes
Apollo 8 occulted.
                      The lunar sphere, newsprint
adrift in a sea of stars, papier-mâché,
or a gray beach mound, felt
the scorch of jets.
Once the ship floated flawless in orbit,
TV sets tuned a blue Earthrise,
a mirage of living water on a slide:
We witnessed ourselves in the moon's eye.
Earth's turquoise islands sparked
cislunar distance; the astronauts listened
to the diamond stylus, to rhythmic seas inside
their dreams, as if shells crusted their ears
in curves of space.

Astronauts circled the stillborn moon—
like Arabian sheikhs, pitched their tent of night.
They logged the primeval homesickness,
slept fitful for our world of color.

WHITE SUMMER, MUSUEM PIECE, MONTAGUE STREET IN WINTER

All day on my hands the scent of orange,
the water of the Thames. White summer,
a Whistler portrait in white, a day in winter
full with black-umbrellaed snow.
On sidewalks the remainder of the night stays
white as shrouds. Underfoot, air-shaken,
you will see it like the past, like the frost
array of white wings printed on stones.
Snapshots take up the street, the distant
sighting, ice-capped, as you write
a postcard, vast and sharp, of something
present—just passing, transparent as absence.

EARTH & APPLES

…"what wings raised to the second power
can make things come down without weight?"
—Simone Weil, Gravity and Grace

Falling to earth in the orchard
with fruit called magical,
my palms, stinging, cup that touch
of apple left from memories (secret
shaped upon the hand's breadth
and fitted inside each fist).

Falling to earth in apples,
my hat lifts off into space.
Tilted over the landscape of grass,
branches stir, leaves
begin twirling
transformed by the invisible.

Whatever shook the ladder sent us
falling, fruit and flesh,
to light on the surface of the earth.
What, in passing, I have shaken
also is ransom for this flight
through air and hurtling of spheres—

The absence of anything is touched
in apples, anything is possible:
that there could be a bouncing
in place of crushed skins, that stem
and core could attempt, within fruit,
a different spin—

that spirit might swing unhurt
when all has fallen or is grass;
that the body, too, might arise,
travel some time alone
and find something other than
this falling of its own.

MOCKINGBIRD

I hear your knock in the chimney,
in the soot where you are locked
by glass. Your flutter trills,
its echo answers from the bush
full of thorns, dark wilted berries,
empty nests. Three frail
yellow beaks blather silent
for their feed. And their mother
is here, perched on the iron grate,
chirping so seldom she will stay
nearly all the daylight hours
before I find her, closed eyes
against thirst. I shut off the house
and open the glass, the kitchen door.
Will she fly out, will she fly? No,
she's shut her black eyes and huddled
next to the blackened heat-brick back
of the absent fire, too tired to budge.
I take a checked dish towel,
flag her across to open air.
I hold my breath, for she is flapping
her head into ceiling,
into molding, but then the open way
her wings are striped, white and black,
the way she doesn't turn back—I breathe
out, look up to dust away the down
spotting paint above my reach.
Straight to her nest, she beats the dusk.

MOTHLIGHT (1963)

Brakhage, the crackle of Matisse
unexpected at a museum's
turn. Exposition, explosive
coloring, unclouding the vision.
Sphere light:
mote taken from the eye's
insight; bone seeing;
to see what the sun saw,
insists itself to be.
Animal lumen, the insect's certain
rhythm; flight dust, its attempt
at adherence to anything other
than itself, to some thing
clearer, defined, sheer.
First lesson:
a collection of Luna moths,
corsages pinned to night.
In a fluster of swatches,
in micro-flashes seen once
from the backseat of a car
as it raced against sunlight—
when colors flailed the lids,
rice thin, like antelope prayers—
aboriginal trances, entrapments
of praise:
this dying lilt, sere death
at the hands of light; disintegration's
luminosity—*moth light*—nothing more;
this nature lore, this shadow
study to purify:
dissection of ear-shattering decibel
beam, splitting itself by
frame, by flame.

WATER BURNING WILLS AWAY

Sunset blazes the mountains, an ice of fire
edges each petal of land as it peels back the distance
shaped of these hills. If we walk down to the bridge
built on a sink hole but holding still, if we chance
to meet for the relief there of talking ourselves into dusk,
the creek, crisp as leaves, a chink beneath us,
will be burnished by the sure-burning sky. This day
will quicken with the lengthening of light, cold snap.
Our faces scrubbed with chill luffa will flush; the quail
vault as a breeze laps the surface of the half-frozen creek,
and our eyes tense on specks of flight. Geese float by,
speckled fish, this essence of talk: it might look to us
like a spreading of blood, the red-lit serpent swirling past
and away; it might look like the end of days, terribly
swift; it might just thrash under the bridge where we watch
the century turn, white in riffs, almost blue, electric.
What we say sounds close to silt. Silence, no matter,
taps out the depths, smooth stones rock clean by cool, cool
touch, and jagged shale skips the best. At the edge
of winter, tilted toward water, clarity sharpens, arches
like a comet, and we know what we mean. One thing is certain,
as we pick through our reflections, pass our hands in the silk
tail of a comet or the rose tint of snow, like ash
we sift, once spun off the icy sphere as it hurtled
across the night: earth rivets the flailing scarf
blown by the sun's strokes of wind; earth splits the trail
at the ecliptic; there is no gaseous scratch
of death. 1812, literate inhabitants cheer,
click glasses of comet spirit. Here, here, if we may
will away the ache of the days like water under the bridge,
if we may enter this stream, this new year, lift glasses
of wine, water will heal the wound of the palm,
may mark the dirt banks but wander on and on by no force

save the absence of inertia—even gravity can be charmed.
So saved, also, are we by this balm of motion,
this conversation, this circle of friends
gathered in the flame and babble, by water.

VOLUME 13: JIRASEK TO LIGHTHOUSES

> *"We are not realists. We are not idealists. We are intermediatists—*
> *that nothing is real, but that nothing is unreal: that all phenomena*
> *are approximations one way or the other between realness and*
> *unrealness."*
> —*Charles Fort,* The Book of The Damned

Jirasek, Alois (1851–1930), Bohemian, novelist.
Temno (Darkness, 1915*),* his best.
Jirgalanta (Dzhirgalantu), Jirja (Girga), Jitterbug,
Jiu (Jiul)—from Mongolia through Egypt
to jive to Romania, the river, Jiu, a tributary
of the Danube through the Transylvanian Alps.
Travel the gorge through the Vulcan pass.
The land is old, the railroad winds
shepherds' schists, the ragged granites ground
to a road. The railroad follows the old river route,
the cut of centuries. We have found our way
by barter, by way of a sharp bend in the Nile,
by swing and syncopated 4/4 time. The way is rough
from Jirasek to Lighthouses, it's a shot in the dark.
Our stops are short, abrupt. By morning, we will blink
by the sea.

A spare light beckons, we move, we want to be
the sheltered flame, center
of five-dimensional darkness. The up and down ways,
the strict divide of sky and water, that curving line
into time, arc of a diver, circling time, space-
time, in space, in time, our minds
moving through the night. Sailing, and the crude lure
jutting vertical, a cone on the flatness of sand.
Our range of light, found.

No one can live here. We think we must whisper.

Where. There's a place
we are traveling where we are traveling
there and there is no place like that place
on earth. Do you know that where? That here, there?
That real sand on real land, and there is water
promised, isn't there land? Oh yes, and fragrant bananas
and water buffaloes, variegated calypso
with purple, pink, yellow. Moonfish, -flowers, and
showers of periwinkles foretold. Hog-heaven.

City of throat slashers, hang onto your hats.
We are moving across the darkness at the constant
rate of one parsec per second (3.26 light years
per 1/60th minute). Unrealness. That is, between realness
and unrealness is the infinite intermediate, the solid
imaginary line divided by Chinese brush strokes.

We'll never get *there,* but no matter what.
The way is rough from Jirasek to Lighthouses,
it's a shot in the dark.
It's probably illusory.

A WILDERNESS OF LIGHT

Remember the moth, a spot of fire
tossed live in the light last night
above the stage, after the crowd
had gone—up there, flung
into one of the heat lamps: tangible lumen.
Its body lost the dust of wings,
dusting down like sunlight sometimes will
core open a spout in clouds, illumine
a single *ailanthus* on a hill.

Remember ibises on the edge
of a saltwater marsh, hung
in the willow among Spanish moss,
part of the tree
like prayers that sing so without sound,
distantly, aroused to flee—
no one sees what causes them to leave.
Sound does not carry here, like a shot
in the dark rings. Ibises, white dinosaurs,
this vision: remember the glossed tree,
its camouflage of wings, its disappearance
while it held still spirits an instant
before the breeze rushed the leaves
and a hundred ibises fled as one,
left the tree alone.

Remember the prayer of the spirit,
that promised intercession of tongues
for which we must remember to ask: prayer
that enters our weariness, our mouths
as breath and leaves, having found us out,
to announce the wordless, articulate
spirit, the body's lone act of thanks.

FIREFLY

When I was a child
on the Wilderness Road
going fast to where my mother came from,
to the place I was to go,
the winding made me sick.
I learned to lean out windows, by sight
send the car head-on—
that sense as if we went straight paths
not taking the hairpin turns.
Clear, sometimes, up fire cherry bark, up
blasted walls past signs that read,
Watch for Rocks that Fall,
my open eye could shoot a scarlet tanager,
a cat-faced leaf, an arrow through a whitetail's heart.

In the thorned locust and beech thatch
were spots the sun leaked to wash my eyelids
with swatches of color.
Light blinked in the open patches, hard rain
drummed the hood, or I would puzzle
blotches of blue space, the quick
reshapings of cloud.

There were things we passed I wanted to touch:
to tilt a jar outside the car and catch some
mountain fog of a morning, or trap a bobwhite call,
a viceroy, a lucky buckeye.
The first time I flew,
I wanted to take the blue Ball jar.

When I felt bad in the backseat swing,
smelling gas mix with Mother's perfume,
Daddy, too, rolled his window down.

Then he'd forget, not use the vent, and cigarette
ash would sting my face.
I'd see the red specter cool,
look through its flicker
to the woman rocking on her porch
and see the pipe smoke spoken forth.

From this moment, if I turned
my head to the fireflies
spun over the grass before dew,
I'd see the flint of the field split from it
in a spell of breeze, see
a tree's twin tops sway as they were lifted
at the break of eventide.

There, as we'd pass a tent meeting
where the voices had risen at once and died,
I'd be emptied of the wish to wear gold
bellies of fireflies stuck on my hands
and throat, to save their dazzle in jars.
Emptied of looking into darkness
for the little lights that fell farther
behind the car, there'd be nothing
I wanted:
a maple leaf splayed on my palm like a star.

ACKNOWLEDGMENTS

I was lucky enough to have been born to a reading mother who lived between books, distributed them to Appalachian children from the bookmobile, and scattered them around me in my playpen, including the illustrated *Oxford Book of Poetry for Children* and *The Golden Treasury of Poetry*. I turned in my first poetry assignment in the fourth grade and was promptly accused of having had my mother write it. This was embarrassing, but I decided to take it as a compliment. When I turned in my next poem to no such accusation, I determined that it must not have been as good as the first.

I owe so much gratitude to my teachers, editors, publishers, reviewers, students, and to poetry lovers and fellow travelers in the arts—all of whom have made my life's work possible. I continue to benefit from a select group of poetry pals who offer me sound advice as I scribble along.

To the good people at Mercer University Press: My endless thanks. If you did not exist, I would have to imagine you and make you up just as you are.

To readers: Any book culled from more than forty years of published poetry can take many shapes. My guiding principle was to include poems that are meaningful to me, in hopes these poems will also be meaningful to you.